Dang

Dangerous Care
Reviewing the Risks to Children from their Carers

Ann Hagell

UNIVERSITY OF WESTMINSTER

PSI is a wholly owned subsidiary of the University of Westminster

© Policy Studies Institute, Ann Hagell and
The Bridge Child Care Development Service, 1998

All rights reserved. No part of this publication may be reproduced, stored in a retrieval system or transmitted in any form or by any means, electronic or otherwise, without the prior permission of the copyright holder.

A CIP catalogue record of this book is available from the British Library.

ISBN 0 85374 745 8
PSI Report No. 858

Typeset by PCS Mapping & DTP, Newcastle upon Tyne
Printed by Page Bros, Norwich

Policy Studies Institute is one of Europe's leading research organisations undertaking studies of economic, industrial and social policy and the workings of political institutions. The Institute is a registered charity and is not associated with any political party, pressure group or commercial interest.

For further information contact
Policy Studies Institute, 100 Park Village East, London NW1 3SR
Tel: 0171 468 0468 Fax: 0171 388 0914 Email: pubs@psi.org.uk

Contents

Preface and Acknowledgements   ix

1. Introduction   1
   Definitional Issues   3
      Children   3
      Abuse   4
      Risk and Danger   5
   Key Questions About what is Meant by Danger and Dangerousness   7
   Aiming for a Multidisciplinary Approach   10
   Key Areas of Conflict in the Risk and Dangerousness Literature   13
      Situational Factors   14
      The Victim   14
      Degree of Possible Accuracy   15
   Clinical Versus Actuarial Approaches to Risk Assessment   16
   Conclusion   18

2. Brief Review of the Effects of Abuse: In Danger of What?   19
   Introduction   19
   Severity of Abuse and the Range of Outcomes   20
   Characteristics of Abuse Leading to Serious Harm   21
      Abuse that Damages Attachments   22
      Acute Versus Chronic Abuse   23
      The Severity of Abuse   23
   What Types of Outcomes can be Expected?   24
   Mediating Factors   28
   Conclusion   29

3.	**Methodological and Ethical Considerations**	**31**
	Methodological Problems	31
	Predictions – How Good Can They be?	33
	Studies of Prediction in the Child Protection Literature	35
	Who Should do the Predicting?	36
	Ethical Issues	37
	Labelling and the Consequences of False Positive/	
	False Negative Identification	38
	Civil Liberties and Individual Rights Versus Child	
	Protection	38
	Conclusion	40
4.	**Information about Perpetrators**	**41**
	Past Behaviours, Events and History	42
	Previous Violence and Criminal Offending	42
	Demographic Factors	44
	Past Mental Health and Personality Disorders	45
	Personal History	47
	Other Factors	48
	Current Risk Factors	48
	Substance Abuse	48
	Current Symptomatology	50
	Personal Factors	51
	The Decision to Use Violence	53
	Perceptions of Children	54
	Triggering Events	54
	Linking Different Risk Factors with Different Types of	
	Dangerousness	55
	Issues Arising	56
5.	**Victimisation Studies, Relations with the Perpetrator**	
	and Situational Factors	**59**
	Risk Factors Relating to the Victims	59
	Characteristics of the Children in Danger	59
	The Role of the Child's Own Account	61
	Situational Factors	62
	Family Problems and Social Support	62
	Socioeconomic Stresses	63
	Access to the Child	64
	The Organisational Contribution	64
	Development of Interactional Perspectives	66

6.	**Existing Instruments and Schemes for Assessment and Prediction**	**69**
	Existing UK Procedures for Assessing Carers	71
	What is Needed from a New Tool?	72
	The Importance of Evaluation	73
7.	**Reducing Risk**	**75**
	What is Known about Reducing Dangerousness?	75
	Risk Management	77
	Key Factors in Training Programmes for Professionals	
	Assisting Dangerousness	78
	Decision-making	79
	Prediction	80
	Bias and Disadvantage	80
	Organisational Context	81
8.	**Summary and Conclusions**	**83**
	Summary of Key Findings	83
	Conclusions	86

Bibliography   *89*

Preface and Acknowledgements

This summary of research literature was funded by the Bridge Child Care Development Service as part of their 'Dangerous Care' project. While the final aim of the Bridge's project was to develop training and practical tools for use by Local Authorities (see Jeyarajah Dent 1998), a crucial first step in the process was the identification of key issues in the field and assessment of what was already known about 'dangerousness' in this regard. This literature review was thus designed initially to inform the work of the Bridge on developing a new schedule for use in assessing and predicting dangerousness in child carers.

It was obvious from the outset that this was a rather controversial area, both from the perspective of practitioners in child protection and also – perhaps more so – for academics writing in criminology, sociology, psychology and psychiatry. I have made reference to the main issues that cause problems, but this review was undertaken with the assumption that people are, and have to be, assessing danger in real world situations (in whatever terms this is referred to), that the literature should be able to contribute to and inform this practice, and that practice should be academically-based to improve standards and accuracy. The key question is how can we draw practical and meaningful inferences from the vast quantity of available information? Can the different disciplines and approaches be drawn together to develop standards and contribute to good practice?

Resources and time constraints limit even the most systematic and thorough reviews, and in this case I would not argue that this presents a definitive picture of the field. Inevitably this book represents a rather personal trawl though the literature. However, I have aimed to highlight key avenues of research and to identify key works, even if each piece of relevant work could not be described in detail. Quite apart from time constraints, the quantity of material available on related topics of mental health, child abuse, dangerousness and criminal careers made this a difficult task. As a result, some rules were applied about the information in which we were interested:

- The child is the primary focus of interest, and I have tried to concentrate on literature that, if not directly relevant, has inferences for child care situations.

- In the Bridge's Dangerous Care project, and in this book, we decided to focus on the more extreme end of violence and dangerousness.
- The settings about which we have been most interested to learn are those involving birth, adoptive and foster parents. The issues concerning threat to the children in residential care are rather different, given the very different legal and situational factors, and the literature is very limited. As a result, very little was included on danger in state-provided residential care.

The balance of work in this area has leaned towards predicting violence and sexual abuse, rather than on neglect and emotional abuse, and inevitably this is reflected in this report. This is not a judgement of comparative danger, but it is simply that the first two have proved easier to study, and consequently far more has been written about them than the last two, at least from the perspective of assessing and predicting harm to children.

The intended audience for this report is primarily social workers, but also probation workers, the police, practitioners in the criminal justice system, and mental health workers, all of whom are in the business of reducing risk and improving interventions. Drawing together lessons from these different disciplines is one of the main aims of this review, and so we hope it will prove useful to people not directly involved in child protection, as well as those who are.

I have conducted this review in constant consultation with the Bridge, their advisory group for the project, and various practitioner groups. I am very grateful to the many people who have provided comments along the way, and particularly to Renuka Jeyarajah Dent and John Fitzgerald of the Bridge for their help and constant (constructive) challenges. This manuscript was partly prepared while I was at the Policy Studies Institute, before joining the Policy Research Bureau, and thanks are due to my ex-colleagues Michael Shiner and Anna Thomas for contributing to drafts of certain chapters, to Sharon Collard for her administrative help, and to my current colleague Deborah Ghate for very helpful comments.

Chapter 1

Introduction

Recent years have seen something of a revival of the concept of 'dangerousness' in the arenas of social and health care. Assessing, predicting and managing dangerousness has always been a key concept in, for example, mental health settings (see, for example, Payne, McCabe and Walker, 1974; Home Office and DHSS, 1975; Quinsey, 1979; Monahan, 1981; Webster, Ben-Aron and Hucker, 1985; Prins, 1986; Royal College of Psychiatrists, 1996), but the development of community care has brought threat to the public to the fore. Thus, the MacArthur Foundation is currently funding a £4.5 million research project in the US on release into the community from acute psychiatric hospitals, entitled 'The MacArthur Violence Risk Assessment Study'. Similarly, work with dangerous offenders has always implied attempts to predict violence and recidivism (eg, Phillpotts and Lancucki, 1979; Lloyd et al, 1994; Copas et al, 1996), and probation officers are routinely required to make risk assessments which affect both the liberty of the individual and the safety of the community (Tallent and Strachan, 1995). In addition, recent shifts in the policy and legislative context of probation practice have led to new national standards for practice and increased focus on harm to the public (Kemshall, 1996).

While being implicit in much child protection work, explicit discussion of the issue of 'danger' has been less obvious than in its neighbouring professions. Several writers point to the work of Dale et al (1986) as the original source of the term in relation to child protection, followed by Campbell (1995). This is partly an issue of terminology – a special issue of *Child Abuse and Neglect* in 1995 was entitled *Fatal Child Abuse* and none of the articles used the terms danger or dangerousness in their headings or sub-headings, yet the articles were very clearly related to the same issues as the work of Dale and Campbell. Social work and child protection have been faster than some other disciplines to take on board the notion of risk (eg, Brearley, 1982).

The area is fraught with difficulties, each of which are addressed to some extent in the first few chapters of this review. First, there are the definitional problems, concerning the distinctions between risk and danger, clinical and actuarial prediction, and so on. Second, there is a series of schisms between the academic criminological literature, the psychiatric literature, the child protection literature, and the needs of practitioners. Combining these approaches, and allowing cross-disciplinary lessons and messages to be drawn, presents something of a major challenge. Third, while assessments and predictions of dangerousness are made all the time by practitioners in a range of settings, including courts, clinics, mental health tribunals, research settings and people's homes, and while quite a lot is known about how people make these decisions and which factors are important predictors, there are serious problems with the use of each of the assessment methods available. These methods include those based on actuarial principles and those based on professional (sometimes termed clinical) judgement. Several schemes and assessment schedules have been developed and are in use, but their utility is questioned.

These difficulties need to be paid serious attention, and consequently we have given nearly as much attention to the methodological and ethical issues as we have to empirical work on predictive factors themselves. However, despite the fact that these difficulties sometimes look insurmountable, there are ways in which the existing literature can be usefully applied to situations where children are the primary clients. Working on the basis that people have to make these predictions, and are in the business of doing so all the time, the aim of this review is to inform the decision-making processes and to contribute to the content of new training for these practitioners. The primary aim of any new risk assessment schedule is likely to be simply to improve practice, not to solve the problem of predicting unpredictable human behaviour. This will continue to challenge the literature, and practitioners, forever.

As well as policy developments stressing community and public protection, the context for this review also includes the recent Department of Health (DoH) programme of research on child protection (Department of Health 1988, 1991; Farmer and Owen, 1995; Bullock and Little, 1996) and analyses of the politics of child protection and implementation of the 1989 Childrens Act (see, for example, Parton, 1991). Decisions concerning the protection of children from abuse by families, carers, professionals and others have received increased academic and public interest. For example, there is now a literature on whether child sex offenders are a psychologically distinct group (eg, Finkelhor, 1986; Bumby, 1996); on how it is decided that intervention is necessary (Gibbons et al, 1995; Sharland et al, 1995); and on the role of parent-child interactions (Brown and Saqi, 1987; Oldershaw et al, 1986). With respect to predictions of danger, the literature is also witnessing a definite move away from the early, and somewhat simplistic, associations made between dangerousness and mental illness towards more dynamic and multidimensional models (Howells, 1987; Prins, 1986; Simon, 1995). We begin in this chapter by outlining definitional problems and identifying key areas of conflict in the literature on risk and dangerousness.

DEFINITIONAL ISSUES

It is crucial to set the terms of reference at the outset. The difficulty with any topic that covers families and behaviour is that most of our relevant definitions are socially and culturally determined and, as such, not fixed. The key terms for this review are children, abuse, risk and dangerousness.

Children

We expect the latter three of these terms to pose some definitional challenges, but it turns out that even defining *'children'* is somewhat problematic. Many working definitions define children as being under 16 years of age (eg, Central Statistical Office, 1994) but in research others have taken this up to the age of 21 (eg, Bullock and Little, 1996), and in psychiatry and psychology the term usually denotes pre-adolescent (academic departments of psychiatry relating to young people are usually called Child *and* Adolescent Psychiatry). The Children Act 1989 – which has to be the starting point for this review, being the law governing the protection of children from dangerous carers – defines children as being under the age of 18 years.

Abuse

The problems multiply when we seek to define *'abuse'*. Clearly, what is abuse in one country, or at one time, may be normal child rearing practice in another. In addition, definitions of child abuse vary according to the uses for which they were devised (Skuse and Bentovim, 1994). However, with respect to abuse, the definitions offered by the DHSS (1988) guidance *Working Together* are fairly widely accepted, and we have worked from these. These define child abuse as harm to children by parents or carers either by direct acts, or by a failure to provide proper care, or both. Despite the fact that much overlap between categories is acknowledged, four types of abuse are identified:

1) neglect;
2) physical abuse;
3) emotional abuse; and
4) sexual abuse.

Skuse and Bentovim (1994) point out the difference between abusive behaviours that are essentially acts of commission, and neglectful abuse which can be construed as an act of omission (although acts may be committed because of lack of insight due to parents' own emotional neglect). They also highlight the importance of intent on the part of the abuser in devising definitions, and of developmental trends – what is abuse at one age might be appropriate behaviour at another. In the next chapter we discuss in more detail what is known about the nature of the danger posed by child abuse and the long term repercussions.

Introduction

Risk and Danger

'Risk' is the subject of heated discussion and means different things within different disciplines or departments. The key question for this review really is whether we are focusing on risk or on *danger* (and dangerousness). Our reading of the literature has led us to the conclusion that there are no universally held distinctions between risk and danger and that in some cases the two are used interchangeably. It might be helpful to outline some of the ways in which people think they vary, and to justify the choice of the latter in the title of this book.

One distinction sometimes made is that risk is only ever the chance of something happening, but danger can mean either the chance that something will happen and also sometimes the actual event itself. Thus, in a discussion of the risk for probation practice, Kemshall states 'Risk is the possibility or probability that harm will occur… Danger describes the actual or potential exposure to harm…' (1996, p5). This is in agreement with the Concise Oxford Dictionary definition which states that danger can be both liability or exposure to harm, whereas risk is only the chance of bad consequences. Under the dictionary definition of risk, however, is included the definition 'expose to danger', which confuses the distinction somewhat. To add to the confusion, neither the dictionary's nor Kemshall's use of the phrase 'exposure to harm' actually imply harm. Exposure to some toxins such as tobacco smoke, for example, differentially affects people and some not at all depending on other circumstances. From common sense use of the word, it seems that danger always, in fact, carries the sense of possibility of harm, not of actual harm. In this way, it does not seem to vary qualitatively from risk. When we say, thus, that playing on that building site will put your life in danger, we do not mean that we are certain you will die, but that there is a risk involved. When we say someone is dangerous, we mean that he may potentially harm you, not that he will definitely do so. Qualifiers may strengthen the probability of danger – we may say, for example, very dangerous, or *likely* danger, but we may also strengthen risk by saying *strong* risk or *serious* risk.

This leads on to the possibility that the best way to conceptualise the distinction is quantitative – danger is not qualitatively different from risk, but just a stronger or more serious version of it. It also carries more emotive overtones. The probability of something awful happening is far greater with danger than with risk. Indeed, risk need not imply a negative outcome at all, but common use has led to an emphasis on the negative particularly in cases of probation and social care practice (Kemshall, 1996). Danger only ever implies a negative outcome, and a serious one at that. Thus, the Butler Committee considered that for their purposes dangerousness was 'a propensity to cause serious physical injury or lasting psychological harm' (Home Office and DHSS, 1975, p59). According to Scott (1977, p128) it is 'an unpredictable and untreatable tendency to inflict or risk irreversible injury or destruction, or to induce others to do so'.

To some extent, this discussion is academic, because within child protection, danger will go hand in hand with risk (although risk can occur without danger) – there will be a risk that a child is exposed to danger if certain decisions are made or not made. At a later stage, we will return to the context in which these decisions are made – it can be argued that concern over danger to children from their carers and what to do about it has to be set within a context of a stated policy for risk management. What we are clear about, for the purposes of this review, is that it is threat to the child's wellbeing that is the central focus. We are not interested, thus, in whether people or situations are judged to be dangerous unless a child is at risk. We thus sidestep, as we will see later, the discussion about whether dangerousness is a quality of individuals or of circumstances, because our definition starts with the circumstances. Without these, there is no danger. It must involve a child and at least one potential perpetrator who has a role caring for the child.

Part of the problem is that people rarely refer simply to risk, but talk instead of *risk assessment, risk analysis, risk indicators, risk management* and *risk policies.* These may be rather different concepts. In relation to probation, Kemshall (1996) defined risk assessment as 'a probability calculation that a harmful behaviour or event will occur', involving '...an assessment about the frequency of the behaviour/event, its likely impact and who it will affect'. Kemshall goes on to assert that risk analysis is different, in that it is not a calculation of future harm, but a scrutiny of predisposing factors, personal and situational, which may lead to harm.

Presumably risk assessment cannot be accurately achieved without risk analysis and as such it is not clear that distinguishing analysis from assessment is very useful. They are both part of weighing up risk. Risk indicators are those factors which imply harm might occur – again, they are part of risk assessment. Risk management and risk policies stand apart as rather different, however, as they relate to the decisions about actions that will be taken on the basis of risk assessment. Managing any identified risk is very much based in the organisational culture and goals, and subject to various resource and policy constraints. We turn to risk management only at the very end of the review, but this will be a central concept in actually designing any assessment schedule for practical use.

We have chosen to include dangerousness in the title of this report because we want to concentrate on negative outcomes, not just risk, and we want to imply that we are addressing the most serious end of the spectrum of risk to children. We appreciate that the term is not ideal, and we do not want to imply that we are focusing on individuals rather than dangerous situations.

KEY QUESTIONS ABOUT WHAT IS MEANT BY DANGER AND DANGEROUSNESS

As we have indicated, the discussions about definitions of dangerousness and danger occur in different places in the literature. The first is concerned with mental health outcomes, the second derives from a rather distinct body of work on criminal justice systems and civil commitment procedures, and the third centres on child protection and dangerousness of families. Some key arguments about what is meant by dangerousness arise from all these sources, and centre on:

- Is dangerousness an act or a condition? For example, Prins (1986, p850) wrote 'we are mainly concerned with those people who have a history of inflicting serious personal harm on others, or who are considered to be likely to do so' and quotes Walker (1978, p37), 'dangerousness is not an objective quality, but an ascribed quality like trustworthiness'. Similarly, Levi (1994, p340) commented 'dangerousness is a problematic condition, not an event, and even if the person does not turn out to injure someone, s/he may remain "dangerous" to some degree'. Others have emphasised the critical part played by others people which means that ascribing dangerousness to a condition is problematic. It has been argued that not only is dangerousness not a condition, it is not even an act. Consequently it may be better conceptualised as a situation, particularly if we are focusing on danger to a certain victim. On the other hand, by necessity, the literature focuses a great deal on individuals rather than on situations, and this often has to be the starting point.

- Relatedly, are we interested in general behaviour or particular behaviour? Within the mental health and criminological worlds much research has been based on very broad notions and definitions. The aim has often been to predict general violent behaviour rather than specific forms of violent behaviour such as child sexual abuse. There are some exceptions of course (Kropp et al, 1994), and some writers, including those at the British Columbia Institute who devised the Family Violence's Spousal Assault Risk Assessment Guide (SARA) and Prins (1986), have drawn up a typology of different types of offenders. It should be noted, however, that violent offenders are frequently 'generalist' offenders (Levi, 1994). Nevertheless, Webster (1995) highlights the need for information concerning the base rate of violence in certain subgroups (for example, paedophiliac offenders, wife assaulters) to be established. For the purposes of this review, we are interested in the likelihood of particular behaviours occurring, but it is precisely this which the literature suggests is most difficult to ascertain. On the other hand, in child protection research, the focus is very much on particular, specific behaviours or events but the work is set within a very different tradition and does not tend to refer out to criminology or mental health research.

- Should dangerousness be considered a dichotomous construct (you have it or you don't) or as part of a distribution (some have a bit more than others)? Levi (1994) concluded that it is helpful to think of dangerousness/non-dangerousness as 'a spectrum of risk rather than as a binary concept'. Others agree (Gottfredson and Gottfredson, 1988). If we prefer not to locate it in individuals, then we must conclude that it is a spectrum of risky situations.

Introduction

- What type of dangerousness or danger are we interested in? Violence, sexual abuse and neglect can all result in child death and are thus all dangerous. Despite a great deal of overlap in their occurrence, they represent very different behaviours on the part of carers. Danger by intent (violence, for example) is probably easier to identify than danger by default or omission (some forms of neglect), where the perpetrator may be unaware of the effects of their own behaviour on the child's needs. As we have already indicated, the literature on danger by intent is far more substantial than that on danger by omission, and this has been identified as a major weakness by recent reviewers (eg, Doyle, 1996), but the intention here has been to attempt as even a coverage of the different types of danger as possible.

- Is the aim to predict initial problems or recidivism or both? As we have noted, dangerousness evaluations have tended to be based on samples of offenders or psychiatric patients. The aim in these cases is to predict recidivism rather than primary offending. In some child protection cases, however, the aim might be to predict the start of problems rather than recidivism. In practice, of course, things soon become complicated and it might be that a child carer has already abused other children but not the one at the target of the current investigation. In addition, because the risks are somewhat higher for younger children, there may not be enough time in the short life of the child to build up much historical evidence of the nature of the child/care-giver relationship and so there may not be much in the way of preceding events to alert concern.

- As we have already suggested, what is defined as violence is culturally defined and certain 'violent' acts are regularly defined as accidents, for example accidents at work, or traffic accidents. There is obviously a need for clearer definitions (Levi, 1994). Definitions are vital as they crucially affect estimates and predictors. Some definitions of abuse/maltreatment have been unhelpfully broad (Levi, 1994) and estimates of levels of child abuse and the incidence of fatal child abuse in England and Wales vary (Levi, 1994, Creighton, 1995, Browne and Lynch, 1995). Ghate and Spencer (1995) conducted a feasibility study of assessing the prevalence of child sexual abuse in Britain and concluded a very sophisticated and labour-intensive procedure was necessary using a multitude of methodological approaches if any notion of prevalence was to be reached. Different studies will draw different conclusions based on their application of definitions and choice of methodologies (Wyatt and Peters, 1986).

- What is the impact of legal issues? There is a conflict between criminal justice versus civil standards of proof, between 'beyond reasonable doubt' and a 'balance of probabilities'. It is possible to be more – if not completely – confident about the second than the first, but meeting the first is sometimes necessary in practice where cases may go to court (eg, Gottfredson and Tonry, 1987). Practitioners are understandably concerned about knowing the legal status of data collected as part of risk assessment and prediction exercises, and research methodologies have to be able to address the issue – reliability, validity, and extensive evaluation, are all critical as they contribute to confidence that any exercise allows confidence in the conclusions and will stand up to public scrutiny. But what happens if the data are not validated? If evaluations have not been undertaken? How far can practice and, possibly, legal decisions about the care of children be based on data collected in this manner?

Most of these key questions remain unanswered, but it is important to keep them in mind and to appreciate that this is a literature in flux.

AIMING FOR A MULTIDISCIPLINARY APPROACH

Because relevant research and commentary arises from several, disparate literatures, and from different disciplinary perspectives, the challenge is to integrate the findings and to represent the perspective of the child. The main sources are academic criminology and legal studies, the distinct child protection literature, and child and adolescent psychology and psychiatry.

Criminology has been tackling the thorny question of dangerousness for most of its history, but as a focus of attention the topic has waxed and waned in popularity. For a fairly long period now, since the early 1980s, mainstream criminology has tended to focus on the victim and the causes of crime have received relatively little attention. Some modern branches of criminology have tended to avoid seeking individual level explanations for criminal behaviour and have concentrated instead on structural level factors, which precludes much examination of the notion of dangerousness as a measurable individual attribute, but the topic is inherent in many of the discussions in the criminological literature over violent crime and aggressive behaviour (eg, Morris and Miller, 1985). Legislatively, however, the notion of danger has had something of a revival, witnessed in the Criminal Justice Act 1991 s.2(2)(b) which specifically permits individuals to be sentenced for longer than they retributively deserve on the basis of their perceived individual dangerousness (Levi, 1994). A number of recent studies have tried to explain reconviction rates with varying levels of success (eg, Lloyd, Mair and Hough, 1994; Copas, Marshall and Tarling, 1996; Clark, Fisher and McDougall, 1993).

Within the child protection literature, the concept of dangerousness is the subject of considerable controversy (Dale et al, 1986; Carson, 1993; Wiffin, 1996). It gained currency in the late 1980s, and a 1988 DoH publication *Protecting Children: A Guide for Social Workers Undertaking a Comprehensive Assessment* states that:

> *Practitioners should be aware of the constellation of factors often associated with dangerous families...The habitually aggressive individual can be uncomfortable to confront, and some child abuse tragedies have resulted partly from practitioners avoiding this issue* (p12).

Various lists of specific risk factors for child abuse have been proposed over the years, to which we will we return, but these have tended to lead to a very high rate of false positives (people incorrectly identified as dangerous), and the political and legal context tends to feature much more strongly than in the criminological literature (we have already cited Brearley's 1982 work on risk and social work). There is much concern, in this literature, about distinguishing the dangerous from the 'merely' risky, and there is debate about whether preventing fatal child abuse is a feasible or practical aim for the personal social services (MacDonald,1995). David Carson (1993) has suggested that placing emphasis on dangerousness is 'danger-

11

ously myopic both in its conceptual coverage of the issues and in its treatment of the processes involved in making assessments' (p51). On the other hand, the opposite has also been argued – that primary prevention is so difficult that resources should be focused on secondary prevention or damage limitation in more serious or repeated cases (Rodwell and Chambers, 1992). Inevitably, given the legal and ethical considerations, the research samples within child protection research tend to be rather small and non-representative, making empirical testing of results very difficult. For example, Fanshel et al's (1994) research is very typical, consisting of a sample population of 72 children representing a range of child protection issues, investigated by 12 workers who volunteered to participate. Less than half of the relevant staff members volunteered to take part. Because of the rarity of fatal child abuse, reports focusing on the most dangerous end of the spectrum are often based on a handful of cases (for example, eight in White's 1995 paper), not enough to draw anything more than impressions. Yet the wider literature from other disciplines is frequently not utilised.

Psychiatry and psychology have been the disciplines to most directly tackle assessments of dangerousness in perpetrators and risk factors in victims, and have been relatively successful in showing how risks are multifactorial and compound (eg, Floud and Young, 1981; Hollin, 1989; Blackburn, 1994; Borum, 1996; Rutter, Giller and Hagell, 1998). However, the identification of false positives and the fact that most people in any category of risk do not go on to become perpetrators or victims remain problematic. In addition, it is not clear how far estimates based on one particular type of sample will generalise to another. However, despite these provisos, The Royal College of Psychiatrists Special Working Party on Clinical Assessment and Management of Risk has produced a useful summary of the general principles behind assessing and managing risk in mental health settings (which translate well to child protection arenas), and these are summarised in Box 1.1.

In conclusion, the main contributors to the development of dangerousness theory and research, at least in terms of empirical studies, have been experts practising at the intersection between law and human behaviour, that is, criminologists, clinicians, psychologists and psychiatrists. However, these disciplines from which these

Box 1.1:

General Principles of Managing Risk in Mental Health Settings

1. Risk cannot be eliminated nor guaranteed.
2. Risk is dynamic and must be frequently reviewed.
3. Some risks are general, others are specific and have specific victims.
4. Interventions can increase risk as well as decreasing it but good relationships make risk management easier.
5. Factors such as age, gender and ethnicity are not very useful in predicting risk in samples with mental disorders.
6. Clinicians should gather information from several sources.
7. Decisions should not be made by one person alone.
8. The outcomes must be shared but confidentiality respected.
9. Patients who are a risk to others are also likely to be a risk to themselves.

Source: Summarised from the Royal College of Psychiatrists Special Working Party on Clinical Assessment & Management of Risk

practitioners come do not themselves intersect much. Drawing some cross-disciplinary messages from the available research should help to broaden the knowledge base for child protection and should also help bring a different perspective to the attention of criminology.

KEY AREAS OF CONFLICT IN THE RISK AND DANGEROUSNESS LITERATURE

There are three main bones of contention that arise in discussions of risk and danger, and these relate to situational factors, the victim and the degree of possible accuracy.

Situational Factors

It is clear that situational factors are important predictors of dangerousness and there is a large literature on this (De Panfilis, 1996; Carson, 1993; Milner, Robertson and Rogers, 1990). Social isolation or lack of social support has often been implicated in the etiology of physical child abuse (Moncher, 1995). In the US, the availability of guns is a significant and powerful situational factor that has made a major contribution to recent rises in the numbers of child homicides (Snyder and Sickmund, 1995). There is also some discussion of the interaction of individual factors with situational factors (eg, Megargee, 1976). However, initial attempts to predict dangerousness ignored situational factors which, more recently, have been given greater emphasis (Hollin, 1989; Levi, 1994).

The Victim

Debates over the importance of situational factors led on to a consideration of the role of the victim. The potential victim is a significant part of the situation and the notion of victim precipitated crime is an important although morally awkward concept which, it has been argued, predictive schemes have not taken adequately into account (Levi, 1994). Many sympathise with Finkelhor's (1986) work on sexual abuse which emphasises that any movement away from depicting the child as anything other than the victim of force and coercion is unhelpful and destructive. Yet, there has been a suggestion that male victims, unlike females, provoke their assault (Dobash et al, 1992), and Frude (1988) has argued that children's behaviour may influence aggression levels of parents, while Levi (1994) has noted that some children are harder to look after, are more demanding and cry more than others. Politically, the notion of the importance of child characteristics has been more widely accepted in physical than sexual child abuse.

In a sense, situational or environmental approaches to violence prediction have developed by default as a response to the disappointing results from individual-level analyses. For example, Prins (1986) emphasises the importance of the victim and the circumstances to an understanding of an offence and goes on to quote Scott's (1977) formula:

Offender + victim + circumstances = offence.

Originally, Scott emphasised that 'each element of the equation is equally important'(1977, p130). Building on this, Prins added 'it is wiser to think in terms of dangerous situations rather than dangerous persons' (1986, p118). The importance of situational factors has been examined by Brody and Tarling (1980); Suedfeld (1980); Steadman (1982); Hawkins (1983); Dobash and Dobash (1992); Maguire, Pinter, and Collis (1984), and we return to some of this work in subsequent chapters.

Degree of Possible Accuracy

There is also conflict over the *degree of possible accuracy* and what to do with the information generated by predictive schemes (see below, and Monahan, 1981 with reference to mental health and accuracy). Indeed, the Department of Health itself has suggested in the past that 'No simple checklist can be offered: indeed checklists are themselves potentially dangerous' (Department of Health, 1988, p12). Some of the child death enquiries emphasise this point. In the conclusions to the investigation into murders by the West family (Gloucestershire Area Child Protection Committee, 1995) the authors wrote:

> In looking back over the material...whilst there are points where perhaps some action to protect one or more of the children in the family at an earlier stage might have occurred, there was no way of predicting that this case was one in which serial killing would occur in such numbers as to make it quite unique in terms of child protection experience within the United Kingdom (p14).

Chance certainly plays a part and has to be acknowledged. The same act in different circumstances will have a different outcome, and the randomness of which circumstances prevail (availability of weapons at the time of an anger outburst, for example) seriously limits the degree of accuracy ever achievable. Related to the degree of possible accuracy is the issue of systematic bias. Such bias may, for example, be culturally or racially based (see, for example, Francis, 1989 for a debate about ethnicity and psychiatric services in relation to dangerousness, or Owen and Farmer, 1996 for a discussion of child protection in a multi-racial context).

CLINICAL VERSUS ACTUARIAL APPROACHES TO RISK ASSESSMENT

There has always been a debate over the relative merits of clinical or actuarial approaches in providing the best way forward in terms of prediction of danger (see Webster et al, 1994; Monahan, 1984). The two types of assessment are rather different but can be complementary. Actuarial predictions are statistically based, deriving originally from calculations of insurance risks, and are made on the basis of group information. Thus for example, the question might be asked, does a person belong to a risky or dangerous group? If they have a number of critical features in their past, existing information would lead us to say that they do, and that many people in a group of individuals like him/her will turn out to commit acts of, for example, violence. In a review article on predictions of dangerousness, Morris and Miller (1985) describe this with the statement 'This is how people like him, situated as he is, behaved in the past. It is likely that he will behave as they did' (p14). However, the difficulty with actuarial predictions arises in extrapolating from group information to assumptions about individuals. Just because many people in that group will be dangerous, we cannot ever *assume* that the individual under consideration will be.

'Clinical' predictions are rather different, in that they are made on the basis of individual factors, involving professional judgement on the basis of an interview with the individual. There is an element of intuition, or 'gut reaction' in clinical judgement, deriving from the clinician's experience, and also from the nature of their relationship with the client. Actuarial or group information need not be critical in a clinical judgement of whether someone will be dangerous, but their own specific and unique history, strengths and weaknesses will be. The term 'clinical assessment' is now used rather broadly, but originally derived from mental health settings where it is an interview designed to make a diagnosis. Morris and Miller describe the central question in clinical assessment as 'From my experience of the world,

Introduction

from my professional training, from what I know about mental illness and mental health, from my observation of this patient and efforts to diagnose him, I think he will behave in the following fashion in the future' (p14). In social work practice, making judgements on the basis of the relationship with the client and the individual case file would be classified as a type of clinical risk assessment, rather than actuarial risk assessment.

The main difference between actuarial and clinical risk assessment thus rests on (a) the source of the basic information (other groups or this individual) and (b) how far lessons learned can from this person can be generalised to others (this is not the intention of clinical assessments because they are so heavily focused on one individual's unique case). However, the two are not necessarily in competition with each other, and actuarial information can be built into clinical risk assessment to strengthen the knowledge base from which clinical judgements are made (Webster et al, 1994, Webster and Eaves, 1995; Kemshall, 1996; Carson, 1993; Morris and Miller, 1985).

SUMMARY BOX

Background Issues

- Danger is the risk of a serious, negative outcome. In this review, we focus specifically on danger to children.

- The literature on dangerousness derives from many sources, including mental health, probation, general criminology, psychology and psychiatry.

- There is ongoing discussion over the role of situational factors in creating danger, and over the degree of accuracy possible in predicting danger.

- Both clinical and actuarial approaches to risk assessment are likely to be important in assessing risk to children and can be used in combination.

CONCLUSION

This review seeks to draw together diverse and sometimes conflicting literatures that might shed some light on risk assessment in severe child protection cases. Despite definitional challenges, the development of risk policies and risk management strategies is being witnessed in a number of related fields, and a new consideration of key contributing factors to predicting danger for children should be useful.

Chapter 2

Brief Review of the Effects of Abuse: In Danger of What?

INTRODUCTION

Compared with the mental health and most criminological approaches, the unique feature of this literature review on dangerousness is its focus on a specific victim. What is the nature of the danger to these victims? It is useful, as a scene-setting exercise, to start with a brief exploration of what is known about the consequences of different types and levels of abuse for the child. We have already indicated that this review forms part of a project on dangerous carers, where the focus is the very extreme end of a spectrum of carers. However, in between those who pose some danger and those who do not falls a proportion whose behaviour does not serve to maximise the potential of their children but where the situation should not be considered dangerous. It is, consequently, not realistic to seek to draw a line somewhere and state categorically that this much abuse is dangerousness, while less is not. However, there is no longer any doubt that serious maltreatment – whether it be sexual abuse, physical abuse, emotional abuse, neglect or some mixture – has significant effects on the development and adjustment of children, adolescents and adults (Trickett and McBride-Chang, 1995), and it is obvious that some characteristics of abuse are likely to indicate the worst outcomes. This chapter will present evidence on the repercussions of abuse for the child, and for the abused child as an adult.

SEVERITY OF ABUSE AND THE RANGE OF OUTCOMES

At the most serious end, the danger is that child abuse can result in the death of the child, although this is very rare. Creighton (1995) points out that infants and toddlers are more at risk of homicide than any other age group and that this has been the case for the last 20 years. In the UK in 1992, 103 children younger than 16 years of age were victims of homicide, equivalent to nine offences per million children (Central Statistical Office, 1994). More recently, Falkov (1996) has reported that the Department of Health receives approximately 120 child death notifications a year. Both these statistical sources will represent an underestimation as some abuse cases will be mistakenly classified as accidents. In the case of the Central Statistical Office (CSO) figures, over a third of these were infants under one year (38 cases) equal to 48 offences per million children in this age group. The statistics also show that children are more likely to be killed in their own home by members of their own family (including step-parents) than anywhere else or by anyone else (Reder, Duncan and Gray, 1993; Browne and Lynch, 1995). It also seems that the levels of fatal child abuse are relatively stable, showing little fluctuation on a year-to-year basis (Creighton, 1995).

The study of child abuse and child homicide has been based on the often implicit assumption that there is a continuum of violence ranging from mild physical punishment to severe abuse and homicide. Empirical data testing this hypothesis are sparse (Gelles, 1991), partly because of the low base rate of child murder. Gelles claimed that child homicide is not simply an extreme form of child abuse but a distinct form of behaviour that requires separate explanations, and others have also indicated that the relationship between child homicide and child abuse is complex (Browne and Lynch 1995; Hallet and Birchall, 1992). According to these theories, homicide is a well defined act while child abuse is usually seen as a process, which if unchecked can occasionally end in death. However, the current state of the information is not such that we can be conclusive about the distinctions between homicide and abuse, and both are bound to be rather complicated and, at the minimum, overlapping to some degree.

Between child death at one end of the spectrum, and no consequences of abuse at the other (if this is ever the case), however, lies a wide range of outcomes. Abuse, while not always resulting in death, can present very serious danger to children in other ways. Lesser physical injuries is one obvious danger, but the less obvious outcomes include permanent damage to the child's ability to relate to other people. Most abused and neglected children suffer harm from exposure to continual distorted family interactions, not just from isolated or sequential acts of physical violence. It is also important to note that many children show a reaction to witnessing violence similar to that of having been abused themselves (Fantuzzo, DePaola, Lambert and Martino, 1991; Hurley and Jaffe, 1990). Just being in an abusive environment might be dangerous. The relationship between familial adult homicide and child abuse is described, with research findings, in Harris Hendricks, Black and Kaplan (1993) and the effect on siblings is touched on by Reder and Fitzpatrick (1995).

The outcome of physical and emotional abuse is very likely to be influenced by the nature and severity of that abuse and neglect. Severity of abuse is usually described in terms of duration, frequency, age of onset of abuse and use of force. As Skuse and Bentovim (1994) point out, attempts to try and draw specific cause and effect links between histories of neglect, emotional and physical abuse and outcomes have less practical value than might be expected, probably because most children have been subjected to more than one form of maltreatment. There is, however, no doubt that it is the psychological aspects of maltreatment rather than the physical aspects that are at the core of negative developmental outcomes to children (Claussen and Crittenden, 1991) and that the psychological consequences of abuse are often the most profound and enduring (Garbarino and Vondra, 1987).

CHARACTERISTICS OF ABUSE LEADING TO SERIOUS HARM

Several researchers have attempted to identify key aspects of abuse that lead to the most serious types of harm. It is simply not possible to do justice to this literature here, and only a flavour can be presented, but some of the main themes are clear. Most of the recent research in this area has been on sexual abuse (Doyle, 1996) but it seems likely that some of the findings will generalise to other types of abuse as well. In addition, as was suggested above, with most of the cases at the extreme end of the potential danger spectrum, types of abuse will occur together and overlap.

Abuse that Damages Attachments

Theories concerned with emotional development of children suggest that abuse of any type, but particularly from a parent or primary carer, will have an impact on the child's emotional wellbeing. The family context in which the abuse takes place is likely to be crucial (for example, in relation to sexual abuse, see Bagley and Thurston, 1996). According to attachment theory and research, the child's expectations of adult availability and responsiveness are generalisations developed during infancy and toddlerhood through interaction with their primary attachment figure (Crittenden and Ainsworth, 1989). It is within this framework, built from thousands of repeated interactions between carers and their children, that children's emotional, intellectual and physical needs are met – or not (Barnard et al, 1989). Research has established that positive quality interactions during early childhood tend to be linked to the child's subsequent intellectual and language capacities and to more secure attachments to primary care givers (Bell and Ainsworth, 1972; Morisset et al, 1990). Insensitive, unresponsive and rejecting parenting during the first year in life results in an insecure attachment relationship between an infant and his/her parents (Ainsworth, 1979). In turn, an insecure attachment has been found to predict later impairments in a number of stage-specific child tasks and competencies. When the attachment is also defined as disorganised or disoriented, such as that associated with abuse and neglect, the child's subsequent relationships outside the home, generalised from his/her early relationships, will be distorted, leading to abnormal patterns of social interaction (Sroufe et al, 1983). Given the evidence provided by this research it is not surprising that it is usually an observation made about the child or his/her behaviour in relation to others which results in the activation of the child protection system.

Acute Versus Chronic Abuse

Mastern et al (1990) have suggested that there are acute stressors that do not damage the child and do not produce chronic adversities and which consequently may not have substantial long-term effects on his/her mental health. In comparison, chronic adversities, characterised by the possibility of accumulating effects, may not allow individuals to adapt and recover so long as the stressful conditions continue. In support of this finding, Mullen et al (1993) proposed that the key trauma causing factors of abuse occurred when the abuse was persistent and brutal, in the home, and occurring in the context of emotional deprivation.

The Severity of Abuse

Not surprisingly, those children who have been subjected to the most severe maltreatment, and have experienced a combination of neglect, emotional and physical abuse suffer the greatest detriment. At the more serious end of the spectrum different types of abuse are frequently concurrent, and many of the major studies evaluating outcomes refer to maltreatment generally, indicating a combination of physical abuse, emotional abuse and neglect.

As Malinosky-Rummell and Hansen (1993) reported in their review of the long-term consequences of childhood physical abuse, most of the work is cross-sectional. One of the few longitudinal reports available (published since their review) describes a ten-year follow-up study of pre-school children placed on child protection registers (Gibbons et al, 1995). Of the 34,000 children on child protection registers in England and Wales in 1993, the most common reason for placement was physical injury (37 per cent). Children in the one to four years old age range are those most likely to be placed on registers in England, with a rate of 4.6 per thousand in 1992. One of the aims of the study was to identify if children suffered long-term serious damage as a consequence of physical abuse or whether many of the alleged consequences were really due to growing up in deprived social circumstances. The evidence from the study suggested that in a generally warm and supportive environment, children who had been hit once or twice seldom suffer long-term negative effects. It is equally clear that even a short period of neglect, whether physical or emotional, *could* cause children harm. However, in families that were low in warmth and high in criticism the consequences of the same maltreatment accumulated in a way that they did not in more benign family contexts. Moreover these low warmth/high criticism environments are not only potentially damaging to children's general development, but are also contexts in which the risk of physical maltreatment, sexual abuse and neglect is high. However, Gibbons et al found that physically abused children placed in permanent families did not enjoy better outcomes ten years on than those who remained with their parents, suggesting all sorts of things at play in the association between early abuse and later outcomes, which simply altering the environment cannot cure.

WHAT TYPES OF OUTCOMES CAN BE EXPECTED?

In terms of general outcomes, Malinosky-Rummell and Hansen's review (1993) concurs with a variety of other studies in considering a wide range of outcome measures including aggressive and violent behaviour, substance abuse, self-injurious and suicidal behaviour, emotional problems, interpersonal problems, and academic and vocational problems, all of which have been related at some level to earlier abuse (for example, see also, Cicchetti and Carlson, 1989; Skuse and Bentovim, 1994; Mullen et al, 1996; O'Keefe, 1996). However, as they point out, little is known about the mediators of outcome nor the mechanisms for transmission from earlier abuse to later behaviour.

To begin with, a distinction has been drawn between *short- and long-term outcomes* of abuse. However, empirical research on the cognitive, linguistic, socio-emotional and social cognitive sequelae of child maltreatment is a very recent phenomenon (Cicchetti and Carlson 1989). As we have noted, attempts to try and draw specific cause and effect links between different types of neglect and different outcomes have not been very successful because of the overlap between abuse types (Skuse and Bentovim, 1995), but on the other hand some have argued that the different forms of maltreatment (sexual, physical, neglect or emotional) may lead to diverse short- and long-term consequences and that it is important to investigate the effects of each (Conaway and Hansen, 1989).

Finkelhor and Browne (1986), writing about the impact of sexual abuse, suggest that the term 'initial' is preferable to the use of 'short-term' which implies that consequences of abuse do not persist. They proposed a model to account for the psychological impact and initial and longer-term effects of child sexual abuse, but the key elements of the model could apply to all forms of maltreatment. They describe the effects in terms of four trauma-causing factors. The first factor, traumatic sexualisation, refers to the effect of the premature and inappropriate nature of the sexual contact on the child's developing sexuality. Children who have been traumatically sexualised by their abusive experiences are said to show inappropriate sexual behaviours, confusion about their sexual identity and unusual emotional associations to sexual activities. The second factor, betrayal, results from a discovery by the child that a person they depend on has harmed them physically and/or emotionally. Children who are disbelieved, blamed or rejected are likely to suffer a greater sense of betrayal than those who are supported, and these reactions may be common (Rogers and Terry, 1984). Powerlessness is the third factor and refers to 'disempowerment' of the victim by contravening the child's wishes and sense of efficacy. Finkelhor and Browne (1986) also propose that disclosing the abuse and not being believed heightens the powerlessness already experienced by the victim of child sexual abuse. The fourth factor is stigmatisation, which refers to the negative connotations associated with the victim's experience. Feelings of guilt, shame and worthlessness may become incorporated into the child's self-image depending on whether this is reinforced by family members and professionals. The age of the child and the degree to which they felt 'bad' as a result of the abuse are proposed to influence the degree of stigmatisation experienced. In addition, those victims who remain silent about their abuse may increase the stigmatising effects by reinforcing the idea that they are different and at fault.

The consequences of the abuse have been shown to depend on a variety of *factors about the child* including the age of the child at which the abuse occurred (Rutter, 1983) the characteristics of the child, including his or her level of intelligence (Frodi and Smetana, 1984) and the abused child's perception of his or her experiences as a victim (Herzberger et al, 1981). Despite what is known about the different forms of behaviour problems that predominate in boys and girls (Zahn-Waxler, 1993; Zoccolillo, 1993) a recent review of the literature by Trickett and McBride-Chang (1995) found that very little attention has been paid to potential sex differences in the impact of maltreatment, a problem that is exacerbated by the varying proportions of males and females included in the samples. Most of the studies of sexually abused children had predominantly, but not exclusively, female samples (90 to 100 per cent of the sample), while studies of physical abuse were predominantly male, and the review concluded that sex differences *within* each type of abuse were largely ignored. In addition, not all children will react to experiences in the same way and more research is needed to understand the role played by so called protective and vulnerability factors in developmental psychopathology (Rutter, 1989).

What is know about the specificity of outcome to type of abuse? No clear syndrome *following sexual abuse* has yet emerged in the literature (Kendall-Tackett, Williams and Finkelhor, 1993). Effects such as fearfulness, low self-esteem, post-traumatic stress disorder, sexualised behaviour and antisocial behaviour are commonly identified as consequences of sexual abuse and, in later life, alcohol problems (for example, Moncrieff et al, 1996). In general, these outcomes are thought to apply to boys as well as girls. It is also commonly accepted that boys are more likely to externalise problems than girls, possibly because of the differential effects of both biology and socialisation, but historically male victims of child sexual abuse have received far less attention than female victims. Studies have tended to combine girls and boys in one study sample, with no gender differentiation in the reporting of results (Watkins and Bentovim, 1992). However, there does appear to be widespread concern that today's male victim of child sexual abuse may become tomorrow's perpetrator. It is true that there is evidence to show that many perpetrators have been abused (Frude, 1980; Kaufman and Zigler, 1987; Hanson and Slater, 1988; Langevin, Wright and Handy, 1989; Beck-Sander, 1995; Briggs, 1995). For example, a comparison of the sexual abuse histories of sexual offenders and nonsexual offender inmates reported that 62 per cent of rapists, 50 per cent of child molesters and 20 per cent of nonsexual offender inmates reported having been abused themselves (Dhawan and Marshall, 1996). In a similar study, Beck-Sander (1995) compared the histories of childhood sexual and physical abuse in child molesters and violent offenders against children, and reported that 71 per cent of child molesters and 46 per cent of violent offenders had been sexually abused themselves in childhood (the proportions did not reach statistical significance). In both studies, the numbers in the study were relatively small, and relying on inmates (Dhawan and Marshall) or outpatients (Beck-Sander) may introduce a selection bias (including only the most serious offenders, for example) and of course it remains the case that a significant proportion of sexual offenders were not abused themselves.

There are no good, large-scale, population-based follow-ups of sexually abused children into adulthood. The evidence on outcomes is hampered by the under-reporting of abuse, particularly in boys. Sebold (1987) estimated that only 10 per cent of actual cases of sexual abuse of boys are reported by professionals and proposes this is largely because professionals miss the indicators of abuse in boys.

Despite being the most frequently reported type of maltreatment in the US, the *consequences of childhood neglect and emotional abuse* are not well researched, and on their own have received relatively little attention compared with other types of abuse. Several authors refer to the difficulties of establishing acceptable definition of physical and emotional neglect as it raises the issue of what constitutes good enough parenting (for discussions of identification and assessment of neglect and emotional abuse see Iwaniec, 1995; Glaser, 1995).

A selection of studies comparing the outcomes for non-abused, emotionally abused and physically abused pre-school and school age children were reviewed by Aber et al (1989). Maltreated children are reported to be more aggressive with their peers and are less likely to help or share with another child than those children from the same background who have no known history of abuse (George and Main, 1979; Hoffman-Plotkin and Twentyman, 1984); less positive and socially competent (Iverson, Tanner and Segal 1987); and less interactive with peers and adults (Jacobson and Straker, 1982). These effects might not be limited to the abused child, but may also be seen in other children in the household – Newman, Black and Harris-Hendricks (1996), and Black and Newman (1996), provide useful overviews of the effects upon siblings of child victims. Main and George (1985) compared two groups of children from one to three years of age. One group came from disadvantaged families, in which several of the fathers were absent and mothers were dependent on welfare. The second group came from similar backgrounds but had been abused or battered, the severity ranging from severe punishment to skull and bone fracture and severe burns. Observations of these two groups of children responding to another child's distress revealed clear differences: the abused toddlers never responded with obvious concern for the distressed child. Most often they responded in a negative fashion. Some became hostile and made threatening gestures or direct physical attacks on the crying child. In contrast, however, in a separate study neglected children were typically characterised as more withdrawn and less socially interactive with peers (Hoffmamn-Plotkin and Twentyman, 1984).

More recently a study by Mullen et al (1996) has examined the long-term impact of childhood physical, emotional and sexual abuse among a community sample of women. A history of any form of abuse was associated with increased risks of psychopathology, sexual difficulties, decreased self-esteem, and interpersonal problems. The similarities between the three forms of abuse in terms of their association with negative adult outcomes was more apparent than any differences, though there was a trend for sexual abuse to be particularly associated to sexual problems, emotional abuse to low self-esteem and physical abuse to marital breakdown.

MEDIATING FACTORS

Not much is known about what protects children against abuse or its effects, but this is likely to include individual, family and environmental factors. In a review of the literature on child abuse interventions, Gough (1993) concluded that there is clearly considerable potential for programmes that enable children to avoid abuse in some way, but that the programmes have very different impacts and the generalisability of the skills learned has not been adequately tested. However, Gough also concluded that there was no information available on the type and range of programmes currently being implemented in the UK.

Egeland, Carlson and Sroufe (1993) studied resilience using data from a longitudinal study of high risk children and families. They found that emotionally responsive care giving mediated the effects of high risk environments and promoted positive change for children who had experienced poverty, family stress and maltreatment. On the basis of another research project, Asdigain and Finkelhor (1995) suggested that the improvement of children's ability to avoid victimisation could result in enormous benefits for child safety and mental health. Children may have a perspective on victimisation that differs from adults' and as such it is important to understand how children subjectively evaluate different responses to victimisation irrespective of the objective outcomes of those incidents.

Conclusion

Abuse leading to death is rare, but serious abuse with serious consequences is also part of the danger faced by children living with some carers and is more common. The literature is somewhat limited, containing few of the methodologically sophisticated, longitudinal

---

Summary Box

The Dangers of Child Abuse

- Child death is rare, with only approximately 100 officially recorded homicides of children in the UK in an average year. However, this is likely to be a substantial underestimate.

- At the severe end of the spectrum, one type of abuse is usually accompanied by others so separating out effects is difficult.

- The dangers of poor outcomes for children are associated with abuse that has an emotional element, is persistent and takes place in the home.

- In very serious cases, the danger is that, if not physically injured or killed, children will go on to develop antisocial behaviour, inadequate relationship skills, low self-esteem and feelings of trauma.

studies which would be needed to untangle causality and long-term effects. But we know that there are certain facets of abuse which make it more dangerous for children – these are, essentially, the severity of the abuse, the context in which it occurs, how long it goes on for, and whether it includes several types of abuse at once. Of the different types of abuse, emotional or sexual abuse may be least likely to be the cause of death on their own, but they could potentially have more serious, longer-term consequences than physical abuse in terms of affecting the child's developing schema for appropriate behaviour in relationships. The literature also indicates that much may rely on the quality of the existing relationships *apart* from the abusive element.

Chapter 3

Methodological and Ethical Considerations

METHODOLOGICAL PROBLEMS

Having defined danger, and explored some of the ways in which abuse is dangerous for children, we need to move on to consider the literature on prediction. Methodological issues, to do with the ways in which studies have been set up, designed and carried out, feature prominently in the literature on predicting violence and danger and have to be taken very seriously. A discussion of the methodological problems is a necessary basis from which to judge the research reviewed in later chapters. There is a danger that setting these problems out at the outset creates rather a negative perspective on the literature, but it is important that we judge the relevant studies critically. This is particularly the case when we seek to draw implications from research done on rather varying samples, and which seek to answer rather different questions.

The main methodological issues include the following:

- What is the outcome measure? In other words, what is the research seeking to predict? As far as this limited review was able to detect, there are no systematic studies seeking to predict child death, presumably partly because of the reasons of low base rates discussed in the next bullet point. In this case, how do you measure actual dangerousness? How can we tell if predictions have worked? Studies have tended to use official records, for example, police records of crimes committed or health records of contact with psychiatric services (see Monahan, 1984; Sepejak et al, 1983), or official records of child injury, but all of these may not be accurate and are subject to systematic bias (for example, Walker, 1995 with respect to criminal records; Creighton, 1995 on official estimates of fatal child abuse). For example, an offender may repeat their offence but not be caught and/or charged with it, or certain categories of people may be more likely to be hospitalised for psychiatric disorders than others, or fatal child abuse may be recorded as death by accident. As a result, studies that include several different sources of information on later outcome or realisation of dangerousness are likely to be more reliable than those only relying on one source, and comparisons between studies should not be made where the measures of outcome were very different.

- When predicting a rare event such as extreme violence or neglect, there will be problems created by the base rate for the occurrence of that event. Low levels of recidivism for very extreme acts make prediction very difficult, and it is harder to make accurate predictions for behaviours or events that have a very infrequent occurrence in the general population (see Howells, 1987; Monahan, 1988; Livermore et al, 1968). This problem of low base rates means that it is very difficult for studies to generate sufficiently large samples. While some of these problems have been overstated, it is important to emphasise that we are unlikely to find very high success rates for predicting the types of events that we are focusing on, simply because of this fact.

- Society is not a laboratory, and for various ethical and practical reasons it is difficult to build up the type of information we need. For instance, some of the people who are most dangerous are incarcerated for long periods of time (in prison, or psychiatric institutions). Early studies in US and Canada were based on groups of long-term psychiatric patients who were released into the community because their incarceration was held to be unlawful (Steadman and Cocozza, 1974; Thornberry and Jacoby, 1979). However, these types of samples do not necessarily represent the range of people likely to pose some danger, and there is a need for testing predictiveness in different settings including the community. New research projects, such as the MacArthur

Foundation programme on violence and mental health, address some of these issues, but in the main it is important to be aware that we may be making generalisations from unrepresentative samples.

- There are many difficulties in this type of research with what are known as the 'false positives' (wrongly identified as potentially dangerous) and the 'false negatives' (not identified as dangerous but who then turn out to be so). Each type of error has their own, different costs, and in cases where the base rate of the target behaviour is very low, false positives are more likely than false negatives. It is likely, therefore, that studies – and practitioners – will make predictions that are not held up in practice.

PREDICTIONS – HOW GOOD CAN THEY BE?

This last point highlights one of the difficulties in making predictions about future behaviour, but there are others and we can only ever expect be minimally successful. Interest in the issue has been high for several decades, however, and as Prins noted, '[i]n recent years, there has been a vast outpouring of material on the assessment of risk and the prediction of dangerous behaviour' (1986, p87, and for some examples, see: Tong and Mackay, 1959; Gathercole et al, 1968; Sheppard, 1971; Kozol, Boucher, and Garofalo, 1972; Payne, McCabe, and Walker, 1974; Quinsey, Pruesse, and Fernley, 1975; Megargee, 1976; Steadman, 1976, 1983; Greenland 1978, 1980; Berger and Dietrich, 1979; Pfohl, 1979; Quinsey, 1979; Soothill, Way and Gibbens, 1980; Monahan, 1981; Shah 1981; Brearley, 1982; Petrunik, 1982; Tidmarsh, 1982; Harding and Adserballe, 1983; Conrad, 1984; Crawford, 1984; Montanden and Harding, 1984; and Prins, 1996. Some recent examples of discussions of risk assessment and child protection include Pecora, 1991; Doueck, Bronson and Levine, 1992; Murphy-Berman, 1994; Fanshel, Finch and Grundy, 1994; Borum, 1996; and Jagannathan and Camasso, 1996).

The 'first generation' of research on the prediction of violent behaviour called into question the intuitive clinical judgements which were being used when considering release from psychiatric hospitals. This research consisted of about five studies in the early 1970s and seemed to show in a dramatic way that psychiatrists and psychologists were vastly overrated as predictors of violence (for example, Monahan, 1984). Following the pessimism these studies generated, a second generation of thought on violence prediction has begun to emerge which emphasises that while little is known about how accurately violent behaviour can be predicted, it may be possible to predict it accurately enough to be useful in some policy decisions (Monahan, 1984).

This 'second generation' of thought is characterised by a clear emphasis on the limits of existing knowledge – 'for a topic of such fundamental importance, the existing research base is remarkably shallow' (Monahan, 1984, p11). While the earlier studies only dealt with clinical prediction in long-term custodial institutions, other forms of prediction, emphasising actuarial methods, and other settings eg community settings, have been largely unexplored but might lead to an increase in accuracy. As Monahan has noted '…it is precisely these other forms of and settings for prediction that are the most promising candidates for a workable level of predictive accuracy' (1984, p11). Leading on from this, there is guarded optimism that some improvement in predictive accuracy is possible. For example, several scales on an instrument called the Brief Psychiatric Rating Scale have been found to significantly distinguish between patients predicted to be violent and those predicted not to be. As Monahan wrote, 'there may indeed be a ceiling on the level of accuracy that can ever be expected of the clinical prediction of violent behaviour. That ceiling, however, may be closer to 50 per cent than to 5 per cent among some groups of clinical interest' (1984, p11).

While some are thus positive that more is possible in (at least) violent prediction, (Monahan, 1984; Sepejak et al, 1983), it remains the case that research does not lend much support to such optimism. One problem with trying to explain and predict violence is that while studies try to identify predictor variables they seldom generate a causal account which makes sense of non-violent as well as violent behaviour. On one level if prediction is the sole aim, causal explanation is not required. But there is a danger that without a strong theoretical basis, correlates may simply indicate spurious relationships which actually do not mean anything much (Levi, 1994). In one example of a study which sought to identify predictors of violence, Menzies et al (1994) developed sophisticated predictors of dangerousness which included measures of personality attributes, situational variables, perceived facilitators and inhibitors of violence, levels of rater's confidence and global estimates of dangerousness to self and others (ie much more sophisticated than first generation research). On the basis of their work, they concluded that:

> *On the crucial question – namely, whether experts or instruments can reliably and validly differentiate between potentially violent and innocuous human subjects – the overwhelming body of empirical evidence remains highly equivocal. Apart from the long standing and relatively prosaic presumption, borne out by various research efforts, that young males with violent histories are more likely than others to remain violent (and to be especially high risks in provocative environments and in close temporal-spatial proximity to aggressive episodes), into the 1990s there continues to be a dearth of statistically verifiable and clinically operational assessment criteria...the objective of a standardised, reliable, generalisable set of criteria for dangerousness prediction in law and mental health is still an elusive and distant objective. And there are no guarantees that it will ever be attained. The overall pattern of results yielded from our METFORS research, both in its original form and in the elaborated replication described in this article, has increasingly led us to embrace these generally pessimistic conclusions.* (1994, p25)

The pendulum swings, therefore, from pessimism, through limited optimism, and back to pessimism, and much of the pessimism is based on the poor performance of risk assessment schedules. It has to be acknowledged that Prins' (1986) conclusion that, 'despite a vast literature ... one has to conclude that there are no reliable actuarial and statistical devices as yet that can predict with any degree of certainty the likelihood of dangerous behaviour', is widely shared (Levi, 1994; Department of Health, 1988, 1991).

Studies of Prediction in the Child Protection Literature

While the general prediction research literature is equivocal, there is also the additional and rather different problem that reports of child death enquiries tend to generate a myth about the predictability of child abuse. In the case of Jasmine Beckford, for example, the report into her death concluded that her death was both 'predictable and preventable'. None of this goes to say, however, that current child protection practice in risk assessment and risk management could not be improved with an injection of actuarial and clinical knowledge, but to aim to achieve this by simply relying on a new stand-alone schedule is likely to be over-ambitious.

There is a developing literature within child protection not so much on prediction, but on the role of risk assessment in changing (reducing) child protection case loads (for example, Doueck, Bronson and Levine, 1992; Doueck, Levine and Bronson, 1993; Jagannathan and Camasso, 1996; Fanshel, Finch and Grundy, 1994) but the results are rather equivocal and conclusions such as this from English and Pecora (1994) are not uncommon: 'Research on risk assessment confirms the lack of conceptual clarity and the difficulty of incorporating it into a child protection service system...' (p451). We will return to the issues raised by these studies in Chapter 7, but in the context of methodolgical issues it is important to point out that few large-scale studies exist, and, at least in the UK, there has been a culture of resistance to measures and scales which may have made developments more difficult.

WHO SHOULD DO THE PREDICTING?

Are some disciplines or some professionals better at predicting dangerousness than others? The answer to this is not clear. In a study of the accuracy of predictions of dangerousness, Sepejak et al (1983) did conclude that the ability to predict dangerousness varied according to profession – psychiatrists and psychologists were the most accurate, but the predictions of nurses and social workers were little different to those expected by chance. While there was a significant relationship between predicted and actual violence for psychiatrists and psychologists, this was not the case for the aggregated 'team' score. Even within the psychiatrists there was considerable range of predictive accuracy. Conflicting results were reported by Menzies et al (1994) who concluded that with the possible exception of non-presiding psychiatrists, there was no indication that professionals fared better than non-clinical raters. In fact, lay persons demonstrated better accuracy than lead psychiatrists in their application of the team's risk assessment schedule. Once again, however, there was much variability within professions and some clinicians did produce more accurate predictions than others. In a re-analysis of the results of 58 datasets from 44 published studies of violence prediction, Mossman (1994) concluded that many of the problems with deciding whether mental health professionals' predictions were significantly more accurate than chance arose from problems that have already been discussed concerning the low base rates of violence and biases in favour of certain outcomes. When these were taken account of, professionals' clinical judgements were better than chance, but even so, predictions based on previous behaviour (without additional clinical judgements) were the most accurate of all.

ETHICAL ISSUES

There is no way of escaping the fact that predicting danger is for the purposes of controlling behaviour by punishment, treatment or confinement, and the aim is to prevent the occurrence of other incidents (Limandri and Sheridan, 1995). In addition, while much of the literature on risk deals with placement of adults back in society, in child protection the decision often concerns the removal of children from the home. Thus, as Kelly and Milner (1996) have recently summarised, choices in child protection are invariably between unattractive courses of action. They quoted Blom Cooper's comments in the report on Jasmine Beckford's death, where he wrote 'The issues involved are rarely simple, and the choice facing social workers is often not between a wholly satisfactory family setting and an idyllic alternative, but that the choice is between two imperfect and uncertain options' (London Borough of Brent, 1987, cited in Kelly and Milner 1996, p97). Getting it wrong – and even getting it right – obviously both have associated ethical problems.

Labelling, and the Consequences of False Positive/False Negative Identifications

Being wrongly identified as potentially dangerous could have multiple negative implications. It is important to consider the potential effect on the self-esteem of those individuals who are wrongly predicted as being dangerous. It may increase the likelihood of actually becoming dangerous due to expectations and the reactions of others (Bingley, 1997). There is a whole literature in sociology on labelling and criminal justice which continues to be developed (for example, Keane, Gillis and Hagan, 1989). In their important study of the life histories of delinquent boys, Sampson and Laub (1993) showed that, for example, imprisonment had negative effects on future job prospects, and because of this might be indirectly responsible to an increased risk of offending and violence after release. The implication is that wrongly identifying people as violent may lead to increases in dangerous behaviour and so should be treated very cautiously indeed.

Civil Liberties and Individual Rights Versus Child Protection

Morris and Miller (1985) estimated that 'with the best possible predictions of violent behaviour we can expect to make one true positive prediction of violence to the person for every two false positive predictions' (pp15–16). They went on to note, however, that a group of three people, one of whom will soon commit an act of serious violence, is a very dangerous group, and the

> *'societal decision, the moral decision, is not whether to place the burden of avoiding the risk on the false positive, but how to balance the risk of harm to society and the certain intrusion on the liberty of each member of the preventively detained group. At some level of predicted harms from the group, the intrusions on each individual's liberty may be justified'* (p21).

The ethics of prediction also depend on what we do with the information/prediction. As Monahan (1984) wrote:

It is one thing...to suggest that the prediction of future harm might reasonably play some limited secondary role in criminal sentencing and another altogether different thing to hold, as the Supreme Court recently did in Barefoot v Estelle *(30), that the imposition of the death penalty can rationally be made contingent upon such predictions. As Justice Blackmun, in dissent, noted, 'In the present state of psychiatric knowledge, this is too much for me' (1984, 13).*

Morris and Miller (1985) argued that it is proper that the dangerousness of the group is taken into account in sentencing, providing that no individual is sentenced to longer than s/he otherwise would have

---

SUMMARY BOX

Methodological and Ethical Constraints

- Various methodological shortfalls in the available research literature mean that care should be taken when generalising from studies to child protection issues.

- Because of the low base rate for seriously dangerous behaviour and situations, predicting these is extremely difficult and 'false positives' are likely, which is when danger is predicted but does not exist or happen.

- Risk assessment schedules have a poor history of predictive validity and the literature reflects much scepticism about their use. This is not to say that improvements in risk assessment and prediction are not possible, but that the addition of a new schedule on its own is not likely to be a panacea for generally poor predictions of dangerousness.

- Predictions of violence and dangerousness carry serious implications for the future behaviour of the individuals concerned. Wrongly or even rightly labelling people as dangerous may lead to changes in their later actions.

- A balance of harm has to be calculated between the risk of harm to others, and the civil liberties of the possibly dangerous individual.

deserved and that individuals are properly allocated to the groups estimated as being dangerous. The dilemmas clearly vary with predictive accuracy – for example, academics have argued about what level of accuracy justifies incarceration to avoid future crimes (Floud and Young, 1981; Haapanen, 1990; Levi, 1994).

Conclusion

This is a very difficult area in which to conduct research. The issues are complex, it is hard to operationalise the key variables, the behaviour of interest is relatively rare and there are various ethical constraints on undertaking projects in the field. In addition, there are crucial differences between assessing how dangerous someone is at any given time (risk assessment), and trying to predict their *future* behaviour (prediction and risk management), and it is important to note which category studies fall into as the two have attendant strengths and pitfalls (Campbell, 1995; Kemshall, 1996). Assessing dangerousness at any given time is likely to be easier than predicting future behaviour, but it is still extremely problematic.

In the next two chapters we consider what conclusions can be drawn from the literature on factors relating to the perpetrator, children and contexts in situations where children may be in danger.

Chapter 4

Information about Perpetrators

Recent reviews have addressed various aspects of perpetrator characteristics (Milner and Chilamkurtic, 1991; Limandri and Sheridan, 1995; Walker, 1996; Monahan and Steadman, 1994) but we have not come across any that bring all the factors together and discuss them in adequate depth in relation to child protection issues. If the key question is actually 'what do we know about dangerous child carers?' the answer is very little directly, and while we can perhaps learn from the broader literature on perpetrators of violence, there are still problems in generalising information about people who are likely (for example) to hit their partners to those who are likely to hit their children. It has to be stated at the outset that we have found next to nothing, for example, about even the simply epidemiological characteristics of those who kill children (and this group may be different from those who seriously abuse children but do not kill them), except what we can learn from analyses of Part 8 (child death) case reports. This is largely because the group is so small and so heterogeneous.

Bearing in mind these limitations, and the methodological considerations outlined above, a range of empirical studies of varying quality have identified a number of different factors which may be important in identifying potential perpetrators of violence or other types of dangerous behaviour. These relate primarily to past behaviours and events and to present risk factors. In addition, some consideration has been given to whether any of these are specific to certain types of child abuse, although it has to be said that the evidence on this is sketchy. In this chapter, we present a summary of this literature and we have chosen, rather arbitrarily, to divide the risk factors on this past/present split, but other classifications of factors are possible, including for example static (age, gender, history) versus dynamic (attitudes, marital status) as suggested by Limandri and Sheridan (1995). Factors relating to the victim or to the situational context will be discussed in the subsequent chapter.

PAST BEHAVIOURS, EVENTS AND HISTORY

Prior behaviour and other preexisting factors are a crucial part of predicting future behaviour. One of the most common to feature in all the predictive schemes we have seen is previous violence, but other aspects of past behaviour and experiences are also likely to be significant. We look at each of these in turn.

Previous Violence and Criminal Offending

It is rare that an adult who is seriously violent will not have had some indication of antisocial behaviour earlier in his or her life (Robins, 1966, 1978, 1991; Robins and Rutter, 1990; Rutter et al, 1994; Farrington, 1995a, 1995b; LeBlanc, Cote and Loeber, 1991; Loeber and Dishion, 1993; Loeber and Hay, 1994, to list just a few of the relevant studies). In some schemes, a history of previous violence is considered the single most important predictor of the chance of future violence or offending (Blomhoff, Seim and Friis; 1990; Monahan, 1981), although it crops up less often in the child protection literature (for example, it is *not* listed as one of the 'most commonly used risk factors' in a review by McDonald and Marks, 1991, and Doyle, 1996, noted the lack of research on links between domestic violence and child abuse). There is obviously plenty of empirical justification for this view of an association, but the relationship between past and present violence is not deterministic. Many positive outcomes are reported later in life for young people who experienced very serious disruption and behaviour problems as children (Garmezy, 1994; Smith et al, 1995; Gibbens et al, 1995; Little et al, unpublished). A proportion of murders and rapes are committed by people who have not previously come to *official* attention although they may have a long history of behaviour problems. Once having committed a serious violent offence, rates of recidivism are hard to predict, and are very low for the most dangerous crimes. Serial murderers, for example, are extraordinarily rare. Most murderers only kill once. It is important, therefore, that we should not exaggerate the predictive utility of past behaviour in the case of the most extreme and serious violent offences. In addition, while 'previous violence is the best predictor of future violence we are ever likely to have' (Walker, 1996, p7), this could be violence to anyone. Studies of recidivism do not tend to differentiate between different classes of victims and so do not tell us much about recidivist violence against *children* specifically.

In terms of measuring previous violence, it is of vital importance to include measures of incidences for which the perpetrator was not convicted. Although the clear-up rate for murder is actually quite high in the UK – approximately 48 per cent (Farrington, Langan and Wikstrom, 1994) – the reporting rates for many types of violence are low, as repeated British Crime Surveys have shown (Mirlees-Black et al, 1996). Self-reported violence may therefore be important, as will the reports from other sources (Monahan and Steadman, 1994).

In terms of other types of offending behaviour apart from violence, the risk of reoffending is likely to be different for different types of offences, and to vary over time. Levels of previous offending may be important as simple measures of incidence of any offending. However, the relationship of other types of offending behaviour to likelihood of committing violent acts is still in debate (see, for example, Levi, 1994). It would seem that if higher levels of general offending and a wider range of victims have been involved, the risk of some violence to someone is probably increased. However, it is not clear whether this is simply a statistical relationship (the more you do, the more likely you are to do some that are violent, simply by chance) or whether there is a sub-group of offenders who are more likely to be violent than the remainder. In a quantitative and qualitative study of violent offending in the West Midlands, it was concluded that the top 8 per cent of offenders constituted a hard core, distinguished from the remainder by having been convicted of a wider *range* of violent offences and having served more custodial sentences. The relationships between other types of offending and violence are likely to be different among juvenile offenders (where a significant proportion of this age group are involved) and adult offenders (who are rarer in the general population and tend to be of the more persistent type). Specialist offenders are probably the exception rather than the rule, so in general a long criminal history is likely to be a marker that violence is more of a possibility, but again, it has to be acknowledged that this is far from being a deterministic relationship.

The previous use of weapons in predicting whether an individual will commit further violence is not clearly discussed in the literature. At the general level, the availability of weapons has a direct effect on levels of homicide, so that the fact that the US has a very high and increasing rate of child homicide (10 to 15 times that of the UK) has been attributed to the increase in gun ownership in the US (Snyder et al, 1995). Despite suggestions that access to firearms may increase risk (Webster et al, 1994; Monahan, 1981) we do not know of any actual research on this at the individual level and certainly not in relation to the risk to children. In addition, many of the child homicides reported in Snyder et al (1995) were by other children and young people with guns, rather than adults. Similarly, despite anecdotal evidence from child protection inquiries (eg, The Bridge Child Care Development Service, 1991) that formal tuition in the application of violence, such as martial art training, may be an important factor in child death cases, we have not come across any research literature on this.

Demographic Factors

One of the least controversial conclusions of criminology is that men are more likely than women to be involved in crime generally and in violence, although the ratio between the sexes is narrowing in the official statistics (Heidenson, 1995; Genders and Morrison, 1996; Rutter, Giller and Hagell, 1998). Even so, in a study of more than 2000 incidences of violence in the West Midlands in 1988, nine out of ten were committed by men (Genders and Morrison, 1996). More men commit virtually all offences (at least as reflected in the official statistics) except perhaps some types of theft (Home Office, various including 1995). In some self-report studies (eg, Graham and Bowling, 1995), young women reported as many offences as young men for some offence types, but this can usually be explained by the fact that self-report studies focus on the more minor end of offending, such as theft. What we do not know is what it is about either biological or social factors which lead to the imbalance and sophisticated work on differential socialisation processes is sorely lacking. Where data are available, the male preponderance is also reported in child homicide (Browne and Lynch, 1995).

It is also clear that in general a large proportion of offences are committed by young offenders, but in fact young offenders account for a smaller proportion of violent offences than other offences (Hagell and Newburn, 1994; Graham and Bowling, 1995) and the age–crime relationship is not particularly relevant for serious child abuse. Serious violence is relatively rare in juveniles, and more likely to be committed by men in their 20s (Home Office, 1995). In cases of child homicide by carers, it is, of course, likely that the perpetrators will be old enough to have children (although they might be another sibling). It is not clear, thus, that age could be used as a meaningful marker of likelihood of violence to children. There is one important exception to this and this is in the use of the age of onset of violence – a range of studies has now demonstrated that hard core offenders who engage in a high degree of offending (and violent offending) are more likely to have started earlier than other offenders (Moffitt, 1993; Thornberry, Huizinga and Loeber, 1995; Genders and Morrison, 1996; Rutter et al, 1998).

In a report analysing the characteristics of child deaths where parental psychiatric disorder was a factor, Falkov (1996) reported that the average age of the psychiatrically ill perpetrators was 37 years, compared with a statistically younger age of 24 years in the non-ill perpetrators, indicating an interaction between the age of the perpetrator and other characteristics such as their mental state.

Past Mental Health and Personality Disorders

What is the role of past episodes of, for example, depression or schizophrenia on adult adjustment? Past mental health has a long history as an indicator of adult adjustment (see, for example, Modestin and Ammann, 1995; Harrington et al, 1991) and is frequently included in child protection studies (for example, McDonald and Marks, 1991, cited seven child protection instruments including parental mental health as a risk factor). There is certainly a vast literature on violence and mental disorder (eg, Bowden, 1996; Monahan and Steadman, 1994; Steadman, 1983; Soothill et al, 1980; Quinsey, 1979; Steadman and Cocozza, 1974, to list just a few) although the relationship is not direct or obvious. Personality disorders (for example, psychopathy) may be particularly important, as might multiple diagnoses (Swanson et al, 1990), but even so predictions are usually rather low, in the region of 20 to 25 per cent who will go on to be violent. The mentally ill are usually more a risk to themselves than to others (Bowden, 1996).

The role of psychopathy as a risk factor for violence has been recently discussed by Hart et al (1994). Psychopathy was defined as a personality disorder which led people to characteristic ways of perceiving and relating to the world, which started early and persisted through adult life, accompanied by pervasive social dysfunction. Hart et al provided a succinct description of the key characteristics of a psychopath as:

> *grandiose, egocentric, manipulative, dominant, forceful, and coldhearted. Affectively, they display shallow and labile emotions, are unable to form long-lasting bonds to people, principles or goals, and are lacking in empathy, anxiety, and genuine guilt or remorse. Behaviourally, psychopaths are impulsive and sensation-seeking, and tend to violate social norms; the most obvious expressions of these predispositions involve criminality, substance abuse, and a failure to fulfill social obligations and responsibilities* (1994; p81).

Statistical analyses controlling for criminal history and demographic variables showed that psychopathy was significant in predicting violence in 231 male inmates released from prison. Those in the top third of the psychopathy ratings were almost four times more likely to commit a violent crime.

There is evidence that previous hospitalisation for a psychiatric illness is a better predictor than psychiatric health per se. Data from the well-known and methodologically sound American Epidemiological Catchment Area (ECA) study (eg, Swanson, 1994) have shown, for example, that ex in-patients reported more violent behaviour and more incidents involving weapons than did subjects in a matched community sample (see also Steadman and Felson, 1984; Link et al, 1992).

There is the possibility that there is a mental health and gender interaction, in that there is some evidence that mentally ill women may be more violent after release from hospital than men (for example, Lidz, Mulvey and Gardner, 1993). Providing some supporting evidence for an interaction, Falkov (1996) reported from his analysis of 77 child death reports that while 76 per cent of the psychiatrically ill perpetrators were female, this was the case for only 30 per cent of the non-ill perpetrators, who were more likely to be male. However, this difference did not reach statistical significance and the study was based on a very selected sample.

Personal History

Prior abuse or neglect are frequently evident in the pasts of people who go on to abuse and neglect others (Monck and New, 1996; Boswell, 1996; Malinosky-Rummell and Hansen, 1993; Cichetti and Carlson, 1989; Widom, 1989). Much of this literature, however, is relatively recent and there are some methodological limitations such as a lack of sufficient longitudinal follow-up data. Estimates of the extent of the continuity from one generation to the next vary from 7 to 70 per cent, in that between 7 and 70 per cent of those who had a history of childhood physical abuse have been reported to subsequently abuse others themselves, and the consensus of several reviews is that this averages out at about a third (Malinosky-Rummell and Hansen, 1993). The mechanisms are not clear but one likely explanation is that individuals become socialised to be violent or to abuse others because they learn from significant others in their lives that this is acceptable and normal. Violence may become a rewarding and useful strategy for solving problems or reacting to challenging situations. We have already reviewed some of the literature on the intergenerational patterns in abuse, and reported several studies (Beck-Sander, 1995; Dhawan and Marshall, 1996) which showed continuity between sexual abuse in childhood and sexual abuse of others in adulthood. Beck-Sander (1995) also reported that 92 per cent of violent offenders (out-patients) were found to have been victims of physical abuse as children compared with 39 per cent of child molesters, implying support for some intergenerational transmission of physical abuse but also that physical violence will predict, albeit to a lesser degree, to sexual abuse of children in later life. However, in a recent review, Skuse and Bentovim (1994) concluded that the relationship between an experience of poor parenting in one's own childhood, and being a poor parent oneself, while a notion that receives a lot of popular support, is not unequivocally supported in the research literature although a modest relationship exists.

Previous abuse of children is also a predictor of future abuse of children (Milner 1993; Baird, 1988). Milner and colleagues have developed the Child Abuse Potential Inventory (CAP), and in their research have shown that higher abuse scores predict to later child abuse in a group of at-risk parents, and higher scores also predict, but less well, to later child neglect. They conclude, therefore, that the CAP is useful in predicting recidivism in child abuse but it is a 170 item self-complete questionnaire and thus impractical in most social work situations.

Other Factors

There is a whole world of research on *neuropsychological and psychophysiological* risk factors for developing violence which it is beyond our scope to report on here, and it is also of limited value for the question of social work assessments (see, for example, Raine, in press; Moffitt, 1993; Kandel and Mednic, 1991; Carey, 1995; Rowe, 1983; Barratt, 1994). We discuss the role of impulsivity (which may have a biological aetiology) below.

CURRENT RISK FACTORS

Substance Abuse

Alcohol and drug misuse feature in many models and it seems likely that the claim that they are related to child abuse has some validity (Coleman and Cassell, 1995a; Monahan, 1981; Fagan, 1990; Frieze and Browne, 1989; Field, 1990) but the area is not unproblematic (Levi, 1994) and the causal role not completely clear (Limandri and Sheridan, 1995). A recent review funded by the drinks industry concluded that it was futile to look for a single general model of relationship between alcohol and violence, and that there was no evidence to support the common-sense notion that alcohol unleashed some pre-existing aggressive or sexual impulse. However, for some people alcohol was part of a high risk lifestyle which included illegal drug use and other indicators. There was some evidence that some people were more at risk than others from alcohol use (Sumner and Parker, 1995). One difficulty is that different drugs will have different effects and some may be worse than others in terms of effect on subsequent behaviour. In addition, measuring alcohol and substance abuse is not easy. One of the most common measures of alcohol misuse is the CAGE, a four item measure of level of use and related social dysfunction based on the SADS-L (Schedule for Affective Disorders and Schizophrenia Lifetime version, Spitzer and Endicott, 1975) which draws on the Research Diagnostic Criteria (RDC). Coleman and Cassell (1995) point out that there are rather different direct and indirect effects, for example perinatal abuse might have direct, serious effects on child development, while exposure to aggression and violence associated with substance abuse might have different, indirect effects. They cite an example of a four year-old boy assaulted by an addict in his house looking for his mother, a dependent heroin dealer. In their review, they cite only one study which considered substance abuse on its own as a predictor for child abuse (Murphy et al, 1991, cited in Coleman and Cassell, 1995a).

Swanson (1994) has investigated the relationship of substance abuse and violence in the ECA data and has shown that the risks of violence among those with a psychiatric diagnosis of substance abuse was between 35 and 55 per cent, compared with rates of between 7 and 15 per cent in the general population. This was a severe rating of substance abuse, however. Rates will vary enormously depending on the measurements of the risk factor and of violence used. In their analysis of 2000 incidences of violence in the West Midlands, Genders and Morrison (1996) found that 41 per cent of incidences of serious wounding, and 29 per cent of incidences of lesser wounding were pub-related – inside, outside or on the way home. This suggests that a proportion of the overlap between alcohol and violence is situational, and thus may not apply in the same way to child protection cases. Another possibility is that the link is through stress, in which case application to child protection cases may be useful. It is not clear how much of domestic violence is drink-related (post-pub, for instance).

Current Symptomatology

Similarly, current mental illness (as distinct from previous episodes) features in many schemes but again this is problematic (Webster, 1995), and present psychiatric symptomatology although potentially important relative to other predictors remains rather a weak predictor. Much of the most recent work in this area has been conducted as part of the MacArthur Foundation's Research Network on Mental Health and the Law. Monahan (1994) has reported predictive validity from some of the scales on the Brief Psychiatric Rating Scale, and reviews have concluded that only a subset of psychotic symptoms are critically important in predicting violence, at least. These are feelings of domination by forces beyond the perpetrator's control, feelings that thoughts are being put into his/her head, and the feeling that others wish to cause harm to the perpetrator (Link and Stueve, 1994). Despite the fact that delusions are often suggested as critical in violence, measuring them accurately has proven to be a major challenge, although work at the Maudsley Hospital in London has resulted in a new schedule (Maudsley Assessment of Delusions Schedule, Taylor et al, 1994). Hallucinations have also been considered a major risk factor for dangerousness, but again, the evidence is somewhat equivocal and the relationship may rely on other factors rather than a simple link (McNeil and Binder, 1994). McNeil cites a study of male patients, a proportion of whom had a history of psychosis including delusions and hallucinations. Of these, 34 per cent had injured someone and 15 per cent used a weapon, compared with 15 per cent and 6 per cent respectively of patients with a diagnosis of alcoholism but no psychosis.

We saw earlier that there was evidence that hospitalisation rather than past episodes may be the significant predictor in the case of previous psychiatric history. In a similar way, Monahan and Steadman (1994) have emphasised that it may be compliance with medication regimes that predict dangerousness from current symptoms, rather than the symptoms themselves. It might be that the symptoms of the illness are dangerous themselves, or that not taking medication workds as an index for lack of compliance with authorities generally.

Personal Factors

A range of personal, cognitive and dispositional factors have been identified that feature in risk indices of dangerousness (Howells, 1987, Blackburn, 1994). There is some overlap between this area and the description of psychopathology given above, but here we are concentrating on current features rather than a history of personality disorder. Milner (1995) reviewed the information available on the link between social information processing and physical child abuse, implicating roles for poor ego-strength, low self-esteem, and external locus of control including blaming others for one's own problems. This is an area that has been investigated in relation to Part 8 child death enquiries by Reder (1998), who has highlighted the frequency of struggles over 'care' and 'control' in the enquiry reports. The role of blame and control have also been emphasised by Genders and Morrison (1996) in their study of incidences of violence. Interviews with 79 violent offenders led them to conclude that offenders did not feel responsible for the situation, but rather felt that these difficult situations were something that happened to them. They did not feel a need, thus, to excuse their violence, which they saw as out of their control. Similar reports were made of offenders in the Cognitive Self-Change Project in Vermont (Bush, 1995). Bush used the term 'antisocial logic' to describe this way of thinking, based on thinking of the self as a victim, and taking an accusatory stance towards others. This pattern of thinking had the effect of giving the offender the licence to do as he or she pleased without feeling guilty. Bush wrote:

> *The elements of this logic mutually support each other, ie, because he is victimised, the offender has the right to act however he pleases, and because he grants himself the licence to do as he pleases, any interference is by definition unfair and victimising...* (1996, p145).

This way of thinking then 'eliminates any concern for the rights or feelings of other people'. On the basis of their interview study,

Dangerous Care

Genders and Morrison also concluded that, as well as feeling little control for their role, the perpetrators were unaware of the effect of their actions on others. Most of the 79 offenders did not realise how much damage they had caused until informed subsequently by the authorities. Most claimed that they had not intended to do so much damage, but they also still maintained that the violence had been acceptable and justifiable because of provocation from the situation or victim. Rosenstein (1995) presented results from a small comparison of child protection cases varying by degree of physical abuse, and concluded that in 75 per cent of the cases where parental empathy with the child was low, and parent–child stress was high, abuse was present.

Further research on cognitive distortions has been conducted on populations of sexual offenders. Bumby (1996) reported results from the development and validation of two scales designed to assess the cognitive distortions of child molesters and rapists. Higher scores on the two scales (the MOLEST and the RAPE scales) were significantly related to the number of victims and extent of assaultative behaviour. The scales assessed aspects of cognition that included justification of, mimimalisation of, rationalisation of and excuses for sexual activity with children or assault of women.

The role of cognitive *abilities*, rather than distortions, is one of some controversy in the literature (for a review see Gath, 1995). A series of reports have suggested that parents with learning disabilities may present more of a risk for removal of the child from the parental home than other parents (eg, Accardo and Whitman, 1990) but others, particularly a research team from the University of Sheffield (Booth and Booth, 1996; Booth and Booth, 1994), have suggested that the fact that children are more frequently removed from the homes of learning disabled parents is the result of expectations of parental inadequacy on the part of professionals rather than real parenting problems. Dowdney and Skuse (1993) reported that the evidence on rates of abuse and neglect among the children of mentally handicapped parents was not clear-cut. Gath (1995) lists a number of factors which make the difference between coping and not coping of parents with a learning disability, including other language and communication skills, associated disorders, the social environment, the number of children being cared for, and relationships with significant others. However, they conclude, as always, that the research literature does not contain enough good follow-up studies to be conclusive about the role of any of the factors in mediating the effect of learning disability.

Thus, a multitude of *personality and temperamental factors* such as ability to empathise, expressed levels of anger and hostility, emotionality, lack of self-control and high levels of irresponsibility, impulsivity, etc, have all been raised as indicators of potential dangerousness (Hare, 1993; Blackburn, 1994; Menzies et al, 1994) but the problem with these is that predictive probability is very low and sufficient methodologically sound empirical studies are still in short supply. Howells (1987) highlights the fact that while there are many statistically significant correlations between psychometric measures of traits and behaviour, these are nearly always small, in the order of 0.3 or 0.4, thus only accounting for a very small proportion of the variation in outcome (9–16%). In the Bumby study, for example, the offenders's score on the MOLEST scale correlated with the number of his victims at 0.22, and with the number of years he had offended at 0.31 (Bumby, 1996). However, despite the relatively small size of the relationship, it seems fairer to conclude that cognitive distortions, and other personality and temperamental factors, are associated to some degree with increased risks of later antisocial behaviour.

The Decision to Use Violence

In an interesting proposal, Genders and Morrison (1996) suggest that a decision-making model of violence is adopted to help predict when incidences may arise, in which the perpetrator is viewed as an active rather than reflexive organism simply reacting to stimuli (which may be as they sometimes see themselves). In this way, perpetrators' values and views of violence, their perceptions of provocation, and their attitude towards the use of violence should be documented, all of which may act as a filter between the environmental situation and the action by the perpetrator. As far as we know, however, this model (and the significance of these attitudes) has not been tested.

Perceptions of Children

This is an interesting but still under-developed area of work concerning potential carers' knowledge of child development, perceptions and evaluation of the child's behaviour, all of which may be distorted (Milner, 1995). Key areas include inadequate knowledge about developmental capabilities and milestones (Whissell et al, 1990), and a tendency to attribute the child's behaviour to negative motivations (Milner and Foody, 1993). There is also some evidence from a large study of preventative work with at-risk mothers that children who are at risk of abuse are viewed as more problematic and disruptive (see also, Olds et al, 1986). Qualitative accounts from child death enquiries tend to support these notions, but more empirical studies are needed to confirm that this is a key area.

Triggering Events

Several writers have suggested that the presence of final triggers should be a key consideration in predicting violence (eg, Hall, 1987) meaning something more acute than ongoing chronic stressors, which are discussed in the next chapter. There does not seem to be much research on the mechanisms or types of triggers at work, however. Hall describes triggers as:

> ...*events associated with the subject's behavioural repertoire which are precipitating causes, short-term in duration, intense in impact and which set violence in motion. Factors in this cluster primarily include substance intoxication of various sorts and interpersonal stress. Breakup of the central love relationship (for adults), or gross disruption in the primary family unit (for minors) seems to be the primary stress trigger* (p124).

He later added problems with colleagues and/or supervisors at work causing disciplinary action, attempts at intervention or termination. These are based on forensic research conducted earlier in the 1980s (Hall, 1984), and it is not clear how far they are supported by other research. Monahan (1981) also stressed the role of triggers:

> *A disturbance or deficit in a person's environmental support systems, particularly the family, peer, and job-support systems...*

The easy availability of victims, weapons and alcohol in the environment may also heighten the probability of violence (p140).

LINKING DIFFERENT RISK FACTORS WITH DIFFERENT TYPES OF DANGEROUSNESS

An increasing body of work is seeking to refine predictions of different types of behaviour. While this makes sense at one level, at another it is problematic because of the heterogeneity of antisocial behaviour and the multiple pathways from early problems to later psychosocial adjustment (eg, Rutter et al, 1998). For example, it has been suggested that the predictors of sex offences are different from those for other offences (Vizard et al 1995; Bumby 1996, Monck and New 1996) and rape may be specifically linked with age and ethnicity. It has been asserted that domestic abuse of women and children is more related to socioeconomic factors than other types of abuse. Genetic factors and hyperactivity in the early years seem to be clear indicators of a certain type of persistent antisocial behaviour (Farrington, 1995a, b; Rutter et al, 1998; Moffitt, 1993).

The search for past sexual victimisation in the histories of sexual offenders has increasingly become common in the literature. The 'cycle of abuse' theory has been intuitively attractive to many and has tended to be accepted fairly uncritically. There are a number of methodological problems with research in this area (Widom, 1989), but as we have already seen above, it is clear that a disproportionate number of sexual offenders have themselves been victims of abuse (Frude, 1980; Beck-Sanders, 1995) and while the 'cycle of abuse' theory does not provide a comprehensive answer it does provide a framework for several new questions and areas of inquiry. We have already suggested some mechanisms that may be at work linking own experience with later parenting styles. It may be that experience of early sexual abuse has the effect of sexualising males and that, for some, this encourages them to see sex as a way to become intimate with others. Men who have sex with young boys outside of their family appear (from self-reports in the US) to be the most recidivistic among any set of violent and/or sex offenders (Abel et al, 1987; Levi 1994).

Tallant and Strachan (1995) argue that 'judgements based solely on predicting future behaviour by examining past behaviour are fundamentally flawed' because past behaviour forms only part of the wider picture and should not be centre stage in risk assessment. They point out that not only is collecting information about offenders' past behaviour expensive but that, once collected, it is of limited use. This may be rather extreme, but it is not clear that, apart perhaps from the risk factors for sexual offending, it is viable to propose different pathways to different types of dangerousness. The literature is not sophisticated enough to untangle predictions of neglect from those for violence, and in any case in the most serious cases the types of dangerousness will overlap substantially.

ISSUES ARISING

This chapter represents a very brief, and inevitably selective, review. However, some key issues have emerged from the literature:

- The importance of the outcome. While different perpetrator information may work better for certain outcomes rather than others, the literature is focused very heavily on violence, and it is not clear that we can clearly separate out risk factors for different types of dangerousness. However, even violence is a very heterogenous concept, and predictions vary, some focusing on later behaviour problems, others on criminality, others on different types of violence (sexual, physical).

- There is an emerging consensus that multiple indicators are likely to be more successful than individual factors. There is an increased emphasis on the literature in untangling the importance of overlapping risk factors and various different outcomes (Caron and Rutter, 1991), rather than concentrating on simple links between past factors, current circumstances and future behaviour, although there is also an interest in developing theories for different offence types. The role of multiple paths to offending is likely to be of increasing research interest in the near future (eg, Limandri and Sheridan, 1995).

- Offender profiling, practised in police work, has been the focus of some interest but is probably of little direct use. However, on the

SUMMARY BOX

Perpetrator Based Risk Indicators for Dangerousness

Factors where research evidence is fairly clear that the risks for violence, at least, are increased:

- a record of previous violence;
- level of previous offending of any type;
- being male;
- having a history of past mental health particularly if hospitalised;
- personality disorder;
- non-compliance (particularly with medication);
- personal history of abuse and neglect;
- cognitive distortions concerning the use of violence.

Factors where research evidence is equivocal or insufficient:

- use and availability of weapons;
- substance abuse;
- current psychiatric symptomatology;
- misperceptions about child behaviour.

In no case is the relationship absolute, or the mediator and mechanisms clear.

basis of the Epidemiological Catchment Area Study, Swanson and Holzer (1991) concluded that the profile for a violent person would be a young, poor man with a history of substance abuse and/or severe mental illness. This type of profile is not likely to be very helpful in child protection cases because the demographics are likely to be rather different than those for violence as a whole.

- What role is played by 'final triggers'? The factors that have been discussed are all relatively stable but further research needs to be done on the immediately preceding situational factors that may activate propensities to be violent or dangerous.

Chapter 5

Victimisation Studies, Relations with the Perpetrator and Situational Factors

As we have suggested, victimisation received a great deal of focus in the 1980s in criminology, and other fields have become increasingly interested in the role of the relationship between the perpetrator and the victim in predicting future behaviour (eg, Zedner, 1994). Interactional models are receiving increasing attention in the development of child behaviour problems, for example, and the importance of such models has been stressed in a variety of places (eg, Rutter et al, 1998). However, there is still a distinct lack of information about the personal and situational risk factors for children who may be more likely to be the victim of abuse or neglect. Once again, this is partly the result of the nature of the offences and the low frequency with which serious incidences happen in the general population. In this chapter, we take a look at the literature on risk factors relating to victims of serious abuse and the role of the circumstances, and begin to develop a three-component model of danger to the child.

RISK FACTORS RELATING TO THE VICTIMS

Characteristics of the Children in Danger

Children in families who may be victims of serious offences pose particular problems in terms of identifying risk factors. The relationship with the perpetrator of the offence is likely to be complicated and tangled. Children are used to obeying adult authority, and they are probably also still physically and emotionally dependent on the carer who presents the danger. Their feelings and reports may be complicated by sometimes strong feelings of affection for the perpetrator, and they will also be afraid of interference by outside agencies because of the threat of breakdown of the family and the chance that they may personally suffer reprisals. There may be certain risk factors, relating to victims, that make them more likely to be the subject of danger and risk, but these will be very tied into the risk factors of the perpetrator and those inherent in the situation. In addition, many child characteristics identified as more common in groups at risk may be a result of a long history of abuse rather than a cause of that abuse – such as, for example, poor health and developmental delay, feeding problems or emotional and behavioural maladjustment. All of these have been reported in analyses of child death enquiries (eg, Falkov, 1996, Part 8 reports) and in other reviews of child protection studies (eg, McDonald and Marks, 1991). There is thus some limited evidence that children with these problems may be more vulnerable, but in the extreme cases sorting out cause from effect is very difficult.

It is clear that younger children are more at risk, and this cannot be as a result of the danger as the chronological age of a child cannot be altered by experience. As we have already seen, children are most at risk in the first two years of life, and decreasingly so after the age of five (CSO, 1994; Browne and Lynch, 1995). However, Falkov (1996) reported that, of 39 children killed by parents who had a psychiatric diagnosis, deaths were evenly distributed across the ages up to age 5. It is possible, therefore, that certain parental factors interact with the age of the children. Indeed, when Falkov compared the ages of those killed by parents with a psychiatric disorder to those killed by parents where there was no evidence of disorder, the average age was lower in the first group although the difference was not statistically significant.

There is growing evidence from studies of child death reports that whether or not the child is actually on the child protection register might not be that significant – in the Falkov study, 78 per cent of those killed were on the register, the remainder were not. This suggests that proportionally more children are killed among those on the child protection registers than among those who are not, but on the other hand, some are in extreme danger even if they are not on the register.

Other factors may indicate some potential danger, if they occur in combination with other factors, even if they do not play a causal role. These include physical variables such as being premature and/or of low birth weight (Benedict and White, 1985), being disabled, or being temperamentally difficult (studies reviewed in Skuse and Bentovim, 1994). Cognitively impaired children may also be more at risk of child abuse. Skuse and Bentovim (1994) conclude that these factors may be important because they place increasing stress and demands on parents who may be at risk in the first place, but that these factors may also be the result of or exacerbated by ongoing abuse.

The Role of the Child's Own Account

The child has a significant part to play in alerting the authorities to potential danger or ongoing abuse. Legally, the Criminal Justice Act 1991 allows any child to give evidence in court cases if he or she is competent of doing so. The literature on children as witnesses to criminal acts, including intra-familial abuse and neglect, is reviewed by Spencer and Flin (1993) and Ceci and Bruck (1995). Several reviews (for example, Fivush and Hudson, 1990) have concluded that children can give accurate accounts of events which may have been stressful or threatening, and that they will stick to these accounts and not be swayed by leading questions. On the basis of the research literature and on clinical experience, a strong case for paying attention to the reports of children in cases of abuse was made by Harris Hendriks et al (1993) in their book on treating children after serious and fatal incidences of domestic violence between their parents:

> ...*we should listen to children, record what they say, take them seriously as witnesses and provide independent legal advisers who will speak on their behalf...In a better legal world, children will be seen as heard. Due note will be taken of their skills as witnesses, of their knowledge, feelings and wishes* (p154).

It may be, however, that particular experience with interviewing children is necessary to extract and record their accounts, and further research is needed to untangle precisely the conditions under which they are likely to be most accurate.

SITUATIONAL FACTORS

Family Problems and Social Support

Family functioning problems in cases of danger to children have been identified by some (Caliso and Milner, 1994; Skuse and Bentovim, 1994), and others have noted that the participants in incidences of violence are likely to have had a prior history of discord with each other. In half of the violent incidences in the West Midlands violence study (Genders and Morrison, 1996), the parties were known to each other – this will obviously also be the case in most child protection cases – and in half of the West Midlands cases, there was a suggestion of previous violence or sustained harassment. We can conclude, therefore, that prior incidences of discord between the victim and the perpetrator will be likely in cases than subsequently end with serious danger to the child. In the West Midlands study, earlier disagreements tended not to have been settled and were sometimes connected to the incident of study. While these will most have been of violence by men to men, the principle is likely to apply equally to child protection cases.

Family functioning in neglectful families has been investigated by Gaudin, Polansky, Kilpatrick and Shilton (1996), who concluded that both self-reports and observations of 102 neglectful families showed that they were less organised, more chaotic, less verbally expressive, and more negative than the 103 comparison families. The families were matched on race, marital status, income and employment, etc, and most were single parent families. While these were not random samples, the results were highly significant. As the authors point out, however, cause and effect is hard to establish given that the key family measures will probably result from the same underlying causes as the neglectful behaviour, rather than being the result of it. In a similar way, Leonard's (1996) discussion of social exchanges within abusive families is difficult to evaluate without causal data.

The role of *social support* and social relationships is also important (Moncher, 1995; Depanfilis, 1996; Swanson, 1994; Skuse and Bentovim, 1994). A lack of social attachments has been noted in several studies of violence, and this is variously described in the literature as social isolation and social rejection. Of the 79 violent people interviewed in the West Midlands study, one-third claimed to have no real friends or to have no friends outside the immediate family (Genders and Morrison, 1996). This is likely to be the case of people with personality disorder, and dysfunction in social networks is a distinguishing feature of most of these types of disorders.

Socioeconomic Stresses

The role of poverty, unemployment and general economic factors in creating critical stress levels in the lives of some individuals has been a topic of considerable debate in criminology, but without any clear conclusion (see Smith, 1995 for a review). Socioeconomic stress is unlikely to play a role in the absence of other features, so that where it does show up in the research it is in combination with other factors. Thus, for example, in their study of the odds of mild and severe husband-to-wife physical aggression in 11,870 men, Pan, Neidig and O'Leary (1994) showed that being younger, having a low income and having an alcohol problem significantly increased the risk of violence, as did marital discord and depressive symptomatology. Other reviews have also highlighted the fact that official statistics show that young mothers, low socioeconomic status and stress are associated with increased rates of child death (Creighton, 1995). Trickett et al (1991) showed that socioeconomic factors alone were not significant unless they were also accompanied by controlling, negative and punitive parenting styles. From their thorough review of the risk factors for child abuse, Skuse and Bentovim (1994) concluded:

> *A picture thus emerges of worried parents with little enjoyment of parenting, little satisfaction with and expressed affection for their child, isolation from the wider community and a lack of encouragement for the development of autonomy and independence in their child. Yet these abusing parents also expect high standards of achievement* (p218).

It is important to note that there are distinctions between different types of abuse and these stresses, however, with neglect showing the strongest relationship.

Access to the Child

There is a very limited literature on the part that access to children plays in the chance that they will be victims of child abuse, but it is obvious that the extent and type of access will play a part in the dangerousness of a situation. Access to the child was mentioned as a risk factor in five of the risk assessment scales reviewed by McDonald and Marks (1991), and also arose in a study of 51 child sexual abuse cases (Waterhouse and Carnie, 1992). Lack of comparison groups and so on make these types of results rather difficult to interpret. Still, children left alone with carers already evidencing a range of the perpetrator risk factors are more likely to be at risk than those who only see similar carers in the company of others. There will still be exceptions to this, however, depending on the characteristics of the others – in some cases, another parent who does not acknowledge the risks posed will potentially increase rather than decrease the danger (Waterhouse and Carnie, 1992).

The Organisational Contribution

A number of writers have highlighted the role of the organisational context in contributing to dangerousness in a situation. This is clearly described, for example, in Dale et al (1986), who report that public enquiries often show that inadequate management procedures, failure to comply with statutory procedures, and high levels of practitioner stress can be very risky. As Dale et al point out, any situation where children are the central focus is likely to stir up high levels of emotion, and research has suggested that a significant proportion of professional child protection workers have some experience of abuse themselves, one survey reporting this to be in the region of 20 per cent (reported in Dale et al, 1986). The Department of Health (1988) also identified the problem of 'professional dangerousness', the key elements of which are listed in Box 5.1.

> **Box 5.1**
>
> **Illustrations of 'Professional Dangerousness'**
>
> 1. Social workers operating alone and unsupported.
> 2. Colluding with a family in order to avoid issues or maintain relationships.
> 3. Acting without a theoretical base and without a systematic approach.
> 4. Maintaining unrealistic optimism, against the evidence.
> 5. Becoming over-involved and over-identified with the family.
> 6. Not recognising the role and bias of personal feelings and values.
> 7. Avoiding contact because of fear for personal safety.
>
> *Source:* Department of Health (1988)

Kelly and Milner (1996) outlined a theoretical model of how decision-making in multi-agency groups has the potential to allow more risky decisions to be made as a result of well known group dynamics which have been studied in relation to, for example, foreign policy making decisions in the 1960s (analyses of the Bay of Pigs and the Cuban Missile Crisis, for example). Similarly, Tallant and Strachan (1995) discussed the importance of question 'framing' in decision-making processes in probation and concluded that individuals treat risks differently depending on how the problem is set up in the first place and the mental frameworks that are adopted. It was suggested that difficulties are posed when probation officers are not aware of how they are framing the decisions they are making, and consequently rational exploration of alternative options is not undertaken. While these types of discussion papers are useful, further research is needed on current social work and probation practice to test these models.

DEVELOPMENT OF INTERACTIONAL PERSPECTIVES

As we have indicated, at a theoretical level models which address perpetrator, victim and situational factors in explaining outcomes are increasingly popular. Recent examples (from rather different fields) have included:

- Monahan and Klassen (1982) – situational approaches to studying violence were proposed, with emphasis on how one model for studying person–situation interactions (Bem and Funder, 1978) could be implemented for violence prediction.
- Patterson et al (1989) theorises that children are 'trained' for delinquency by interactions with their parents, which leads to an escalation of discord.

SUMMARY BOX

Victim and Situational Risk Factors

These are less researched and less verified than those in the previous chapter

Risk factors relating to the victim:

- being young (under 5, particularly)
- being premature, or of low birth weigh
- being more difficult to control
- giving an account of harm or danger.

Risk factors associated with the situation

- family problems
- low levels of social support
- high levels of socioeconomic stress
- access to the child
- organisational dangerousness and poor decision-making.

- In a review article, Lytton (1990) argued that children have effects on their parents as well as vice versa ('control systems theory') displaying constant reciprocal adaptation. Similarly, see Brown and Saqi (1987) and Oldershaw et al (1986).

There is some consensus that interactional models that seek to untangle the dynamics of abusive relationships and which can introduce the role of situational factors, rather than seeking to locate dangerousness within any one individual in the situation, are more likely to be fruitful in the longer term than models that can only focus on any one single facet. It is clear that to many writing in the literature, this direction makes more theoretical sense than simple additive lists of risk factors. The challenge, of course, is translating this into practical application and still enabling realistic decisions about family support to be made. At this stage, the important point is that factors from a number of different perspectives need to be included, concerning all of the carer, the child and the context.

Chapter 6

Existing Instruments and Schemes for Assessment and Prediction

For various purposes, and in various ways, people have tried to sytemise their own understanding of the important factors in predicting violence by making checklists and other assessment and prediction schedules. In fact, there is a fairly long history of prediction schemes, usually aiming to predict occurrence or recurrence of violence. They vary enormously, from lists of risk indicators to complicated, structured interview schedules, the latter of which are considered to be the most accurate (Milner, 1995). Some examples are listed in Box 6.1.

In addition to these, there are a number of locally developed tools in use, particularly in the US, where they have been used for many years and usually take the form of risk assessment schedules (English and Pecora, 1994; Doueck, Bronson and Levine, 1992). At least 42 states have now adopted risk assessment models (Berkowitz, 1991). There is evidence that these can be helpful, but also that they vary considerably in their definitions, purposes and the quality of evaluation (English and Pecora, 1994; DePanfilis and Scannapieco, 1994).

As an example of how existing checklist type schemes might work, in the ORBS (Hinton, 1975, 1983a) six observers – usually nurses – rate individuals on four dimensions: belligerence (anti-social behaviour), psychotic disorientation, social withdrawal and personal hygiene. However, in this example, within a hospital population little relationship existed between current ward behaviour as assessed by these scales and either previous convictions or personality traits. Whether relationships exist with post-discharge behaviour remains to be established.

> **BOX 6.1**
>
> **Examples of Existing Instruments, Checklists and Schemes for Violence and Dangerousness Prediction**
>
> - Ammerman, Hensen and Van Hasselt (1988), Child Abuse and Neglect Interview Schedule.
> - Dalgleish and Drew (1989) Risk Indicators.
> - Hare (1991) 20-item Psychopathy Checklist.
> - Hinton (1975, 1983a) Objective Behaviour Rating Scales (OBRS) for assessing offenders in secure settings.
> - Kropp et al (1994) The British Columbia Institute on Family Violence's Spousal Assault Risk Assessment Guide (SARA).
> - The MacArthur Foundation Violence Risk Assessment Study.
> - Menzies et al (1994) Dangerous Behaviour Rating Scheme (DBRS).
> - Milner (1995) Child Abuse Prevention Inventory (CAP).
> - Webster et al (1994) The Violence Prediction Scheme (ASSESS-LIST).
> - Webster and Eaves (1995) The HCR–20 Assessment of Dangerousness and Risk.

In several cases, the schedule is not presented as a statistically valid or reliable instrument (as a rating scale or measurement device), but as an 'aide memoire'. For example, Webster et al (1994) suggest that the ASSESS-LIST 'can serve simply as an organising method to ensure that clinicians do not neglect to consider items which ought to be taken into account' (p49). In addition, several are not intended to be static. Again, in presenting the ASSESS-LIST, Webster et al (1994) state that the scheme should encourage the monitoring of progress over time and that assessors should return to the schedule with new information.

Reasons for being critical of many of these have already been highlighted. A number of issues including reliability, validity, specificity, who uses them and how they are used in relation to each need taken into account when evaluating their usefulness. Milner (1995) has also pointed out the lack of understanding of the role of buffering or protective factors and their absence from these types of schedules.

EXISTING UK PROCEDURES FOR ASSESSING CARERS

What do we know about existing procedures in use in UK settings (which may not be very formal) for assessing carers and caretaking? The answer is, actually, not a great deal. Although nearly a decade has passed since its original publication, there is little in the way of published material about, for example, the use of existing child protection procedures recommended by the Department of Health (in the 'Orange Book', DoH, 1988) or in *Working Together* (DoH, HO and DES, 1991). Similarly, despite rapid development of child abuse as a policy issue during the 1970s and 1980s (Parton, 1991), development of overarching risk policies in child protection work has been slow and the limited anecdotal information that does exist suggests that practice varies enormously between local authority areas. In a recent article, Kelly and Milner (1996) highlighted some of the problems posed by recent legislation when assessing what is and is not 'good enough' parenting. It is obvious that there is a critical need for descriptive information about the content, process and outcome of routine child protection work with respect to violence against children generally (Gough, 1993), as well as for information about how social workers deal with the more extreme end of the spectrum where serious danger is a risk.

There are certainly frequent objections in the child care literature to any type of schedule or screening instruments (Wiffin, 1996) with their dismissal (for example, as producing simply a 'checklist mentality' – Kelly and Milner, 1996) being not uncommon. While some local 'instruments' or training foci have been developed in a similar way to the US local instruments, these have not been systematically evaluated. For example, Stone (1992) developed a model for risk assessment in physical abuse and neglect which included a high risk checklist of factors relating to the parents, case notes and child (such as, for example, parent was abused as a child, or the child was of low birth weight) but the factors employed were only very vaguely defined, and evaluation data have not been reported.

What is Needed from a New 'Tool'?

Different tools are useful for different purposes. Is something new needed in UK child protection? Currently there is very little in this country that is aimed at the very extreme end of the child danger spectrum. Drawing together the previous sections and what is known about existing instruments and schemes, what general conclusions can we draw about the key elements of any new assessment and prediction tool for use in child protection situations?

It seems likely that any new risk assessment schedule will need to incorporate key elements including:

- perpetrator factors, victim factors and situational factors;
- being directed at findings from the past, factors in the present, and probabilities about the future;
- aiding linear decision-making but also allowing elements of clinical decision-making and deduction.

Leading on from the last of these, it is likely – from what we know of other studies and schemes – that the most useful schedule will not provide an answer in its own right, but be a way of *informing decisions* by child protection workers. However, it will need to contain objective elements, and to be useful to a range of practitioners who may come from rather different backgrounds. It is likely to be most useful if it can focus on predicting or assessing specific abuse behaviours rather than broad and generic behaviours such as crime or danger.

For use by practitioners, any new checklist will need to rely on reports of behavioural incidents, rather than on social workers' perceptions of difficult-to-measure concepts such as personality disorder. The literature (and the relevant professional organisations such as the British Psychological Society) is quite clear that assessment of factors such as psychiatric diagnosis, alcohol abuse, experience of hallucinations, and so on, should only be attempted by people trained to use the appropriate measures in a reliable and valid way. As an instrument designed to be incorporated into normal child protection procedures is unlikely to contain any standardised elements, it will have to be to be simple and reliant on the presence of clearly identifiable behaviours and incidents, rather than underlying constructs or diagnoses. For example, it would be impossible to assess 'attachment' using a checklist format, but it would be possible to rate some of the behavioural indicators such as low levels of mutual contact.

The Importance of Evaluation

The contribution of instruments and schemes for risk assessment and danger prediction to protecting children can only be discovered through systematic evaluation, but there is a drastic lack of adequate information on this front about most of the schemes listed (DePanfilis and Scannapieco, 1991; Doueck et al, 1992; Gough, 1993). Many schemes and intervention programmes are inadequately evaluated and thus almost useless. Many have been developed through what has been referred to as development by consensus (for example, Doueck et al, 1992) where key risk factors are selected from the child abuse research literature by teams of practitioners and child welfare experts, but the scientific credibility of this approach can only be answered by whether or not they then work in practice with the selected population. It is crucial to measure the extent to which they accurately predict and protect; the situations in which they work or do not; how they interact with clinical judgement; the other external factors that impact on their success; and how practical they are before any real conclusion can be drawn about whether they are a useful contribution to the field or not, and this would, of course, be the case with any new risk assessment schedule or screening instrument. Without clear evaluation, one of the main dangers is that the introduction of a new instrument may lead practitioners to become lulled into complacency that the problem has been tackled (see, for example, Kemshall, 1995b).

Doueck et al (1992) provide a useful overview of the standards necessary for an adequate evaluation of a risk assessment model, which include the impact of the schedule on the organisation; whether or not the explicit goals of the schedule have been met; whether there are any changes in casework practice; and whether there are changes in client outcomes.

SUMMARY BOX

Existing Predictive Schemes

- A number of existing predictive instruments, checklists and schemes for violence prediction are examined.

- Reasons for being critical include problems with reliability, validity, specificity, who uses them and how they are used, but those that act in addition to existing risk management practices are likely to be most relevant.

- Little is known about existing UK procedures for assessing child carers and evaluations are in short supply but are extremely necessary.

Chapter 7

Reducing Risk

WHAT IS KNOWN ABOUT REDUCING DANGEROUSNESS?

There are two ways of looking at this question. The first is to assess the role of specific treatment programmes, and the second is to look at the effect of routine child protection interventions. Treatment programmes have tended to focus on those who are the target of the criminal justice system and/or are sex offenders. Howells (1987) provides a useful review of various treatment approaches in these cases, including changing the aversive environment; social skills training; changing aggressive cognition; changing anger arousal; ward management of violence; and changing sexual violence. There have been a small number of studies evaluating effectiveness of social skills training (SST), which suggest that it is a potentially useful approach but not a panacea. General outcome studies show that at least some kinds of therapeutic interventions can have an effect in changing criminal behaviour. In a widely cited paper, Martinson (1974) presented a review of 231 studies of treatment in penal settings, drawing the pessimistic conclusion that nothing works in preventing recidivism. These conclusions have, however, since been challenged and the general outlook is a little more positive (McGuire, 1995; Losel, 1995). For example, Blackburn (1980) reviewed 40 outcome studies and of those that looked at recidivist rates, half reported positive results. Dobash and Dobash (1992) provide a review of treatment programmes for violent offenders. The consensus is, however, that the effect size in successful programmes is likely to be relatively small – in the order of a reduction in offending of about 10 per cent on average (McGuire, 1995).

In terms of social intervention programmes, including routine case work, the demands and aims of intervention are very high and the chance of failure will be correspondingly high. Moncher (1995, p430), for example, argues:

> ...the present research suggests that intervening in child abuse requires community efforts to connect with isolated families in a noncritical, emotionally supportive and tangibly supportive manner. Services from community sources aimed at reducing the social isolation of the families and addressing the emotional needs of the mothers should be provided to encourage nurturing relationships between parents and children.

This may be an extremely tall order in times of resource limitation and stress between providing general family support versus intervention after crises have occurred.

In general, while there is there is a fair amount of information on the limited success of social workers in working with families where child protection issues have been identified, at least in terms of repeated serious abuse (Thoburn, Lewis and Shemings, 1995; Farmer and Owen, 1995), there are also studies which show intervention often does not prevent re-abuse of a less serious nature (Cleaver and Freeman, 1995; Gough, 1993). Gough's review (1993) of intervention in child abuse cases concluded that child protection cases have a relatively high rate of re-referral and only improve outcomes in a few extreme cases where children are permanently removed from families. This is partly because there will be many adverse aspects in the lives of abused children and intervening in a positive way to affect all the aspects is probably beyond the scope of most agencies.

Two evaluations of US risk assessment schedules were reported in DePanfilis and Scannapieco (1994). The first of these suggested that all of the children who were assessed as 'unsafe', for whom intervention was provided, were not subject to future reports of maltreatment at least within a six month period. The nature of the intervention based on the risk assessment is not clear from the report, however, and so the actual cause of the success rate is difficult to determine. In the second evaluation, the research focused on whether intervention was appropriately related to risk assessment, and found that indeed in cases where there were the most risk factors, intervention increased as it was supposed to. How successful the intervention then turned out to be, however, was not reported. These two cases illustrate the difficulties of sorting out the actual elements of risk management and intervention practices which contribute to good outcomes. They do not tell us anything about what works with whom.

In some cases, as the Royal College of Psychiatrists Special Working Party on Clinical Assessment and Management of Risk (1996) has highlighted, intervention can *increase* risk, and the interaction between the clinician (or professional) and the patient (or client) will be critical in whether intervention works or not. There is some limited evidence that special interventions, on top of routine case work, can be very worthwhile, but they have not tended to be sufficiently evaluated to assess their general applicability (Gough, 1993). It is important that the expectations of intervention are not too high.

RISK MANAGEMENT

How do actuarial and clinical judgements actually operate in practice, and how is risk managed in different situations? The evidence is that this is a difficult area and one where practice varies considerably but where questions are being more clearly addressed than they have been previously (for example, Corby and Mills, 1986; Carson, 1993; Kemshall and Pritchard, 1995). Key questions about risk management in child protection include:

- How do resources impinge on risk assessment and danger prediction?
- How are decisions made about the 'next step' after assessment?
- What is the role of the organisational context? What do we know about the wide range of responses made to very similar situations at different times and places?

Again, the answers to some of these questions have been more clearly articulated in the mental health field than in the child protection field, although there is increasing discussion in the child protection arena. The Royal College of Psychiatrists Special Working Party (1996) recommended the development of a management plan in cases of patients who presented a risk of dangerous behaviour. This plan should aim to change the balance between risk and safety and certain factors had to be considered including whether the patient had special needs such as limited knowledge of English, whether a date for review had been set, whether the right information had been shared with the right people, and whether records had been adequately kept.

In probation, Kemshall (1996) has also identified key elements of good risk management, and these are summarised in Box 7.1.

Box 7.1

Principles for Risk Management in Probation

1. Risk should be appropriately identified.
2. Interventions should be matched to the risks.
3. Interventions should be focused on reducing the risks.
4. The effectiveness of interventions should be frequently reviewed.
5. That recording and learning from failure is important.

Source: Summarised from Kemshall (1996)

This leads us on to key factors that might be considered for inclusion in the development of a training programme for professionals working in child protection arenas.

KEY FACTORS IN TRAINING PROGRAMMES FOR PROFESSIONALS ASSESSING DANGEROUSNESS

Simply suggesting ways of improving practice will not work unless professionals are trained or inducted into the approach. If a new information gathering tool were to be developed in child protection, what would be the significant training ssues? There is not a great literature in this area, but the recent Department of Health funded research initiative has generated several studies that are of direct or indirect relevance, including Sharland et al (1995) and Lawson et al (1995) and others have evaluated the process of planning and running a training course for multi-disciplinary professionals in the wake of a child death inquiry. Certain areas are likely to be important in any training programme developed alongside a new assessment and prediction scheme. Those that follow are examples of the types of issues that may need to be included based on information contained in child protection inquiries and the practitioner literature.

Decision-making

As we have seen, different types of decision-making are available and in use in practice (for example, Limandri and Sheridan, 1995), often based on a model that combines actuarial (linear, academic) and clinical (deductive, contextual) factors. Initial training on the use of risk assessment schedules is likely to prove helpful to practitioners being asked to employ them and make decisions based on their results. The training should explore the options and explain the development of the schedule as well as addressing the importance of other contextual factors such as fear, or work pressures, on the quality of decision-making.

Carson (1993) has provided useful discussions of the ways to improve decision-making about dangerousness and risk based on inter-disciplinary cooperation, and has highlighted some of the problems in exchange of information and management of risk, as have others describing local training schemes for improving judgements about risk (Brady, Wright and Williams, 1996). A recent article by Kelly and Milner (1996) has applied some of the basic psychological research on decision-making to child protection, and in particular highlighted the risks associated with making decisions in a multi-agency forum. They show how case conference decisions can be significantly more risky than those taken by professionals with individual responsibility, because of the ways in which the key issues are set up in the first place. Cyclical processes begin, so that those who do not agree with the group become excluded from it and risky decisions are built on by the remaining or more powerful members.

Understanding that this phenomenon occurs will be a helpful basis for understanding how decisions should be made informed by a risk assessment schedule.

Within the field of forensic violence prediction, Hall (1987) has suggested that the development of a 'violence prediction decision tree' might be useful, which takes the form of a reiterative flow diagram, beginning with boxes containing questions such as 'is there an adequate forensic database? (If no, stop and correct)', through 'analysis of retrospective and current cognitive distortions present (if no, stop and find out)', and 'examination of opportunity factors?' until a prediction of violence is thought to be fairly secure on the basis of the information collected. The relevance of these more prescriptive types of schemes to child protection work is probably minimal, given the organisational and resource contexts.

Prediction

It may be important to consider whether research exists on, for example, teaching about probability and prediction. Although the suggestion may sound odd, some of the gambling literature may actually be useful here – some commonplace explanations of the limits of probability are available for treatment of obsessive gamblers, for example, whose understanding is likely to be limited (Griffiths, 1995). The full literature review could consider material on the issue of helping understand probability, prediction and the ethics associated.

Bias and Disadvantage

Issues of structural disadvantage, stereotyping, cultural variation and assessing risk within particular client groups may be useful. A recent (US) review of race and child welfare services concluded that there is a distinct pattern of inequity in the provision of child welfare services to black families, and that the relationship is complicated by confounding variables such as socioeconomic status (Courtney et al, 1996). Addressing the effects of bias and subjectivity (as distinct from clinical judgement) on decision-making will be important in training programmes.

Organisational Context

Major issues exist concerning the sharing of information between agencies and workers, the role of systematic recording, how workers interpret and carry out policies, and the broader organisational context. The impact of resource limitations on decision-making and effective work strategies will need to be addressed at some stage, as will management of situations where the schedule may identify problems but where resources do not allow adequate intervention.

SUMMARY BOX

Treatment and Intervention

- The demands placed on routine social intervention programmes are high, and the chance of failure is correspondingly high, but there is evidence that most success is achieved in the very extreme cases.

- There is more optimism now than there was a few decades ago concerning the success of therapeutic interventions with serious offenders

- Risk management practice varies considerably but questions are being addressed more clearly now than previously. These include the role of resources, decision-making and the organisational context.

- Training programmes
  - should show how different types of decision-making are available, each of which brings its own particular biases and risks;
  - should lead to understanding of the limits and uses of prediction;
  - should face issues of structural disadvantage and stereotyping.

Chapter 8

Summary and Conclusions

The first half of this chapter summarises the main findings from this literature review, and highlights the key issues raised. The second half moves on to draw some conclusions and recommendations for future research.

SUMMARY OF KEY FINDINGS

(1) Definitions of the key terms proved problematic, but it was concluded that danger is the risk of a serious, negative outcome. The review focused on danger to children posed by their carers, and relevant research has been conducted in a number of fields including criminology, mental health, probation, psychology and psychiatry. Very little from these fields directly relates to risks to children, however, and the rather unrelated field of child protection is methodologically rather different. Clinical and actuarial approaches to risk assessment are described, and it is concluded that both will be important in assessing risk to children.

(2) Child death is rare, and statistics were presented. At the extreme end of the spectrum one type of abuse is often accompanied by another so it is difficult to untangle particular routes from certain types of abuse to certain outcomes. However, it is clear that the dangers of poor outcomes are increased with emotional abuse which is persistent and takes place in the home. While death is unusual, a range of negative psychosocial outcomes have been reported for abused children, including the development of antisocial behaviour, inadequate interactional skills, substance abuse and feelings of trauma.

(3) A number of methodological problems with the literature were outlined. Generalising from dangerousness studies to child protection work is fraught with risk due to various methodological shortfalls in the available research and much variation in the types of samples employed. The very low base rate for dangerous behaviour makes prediction extremely difficult, and optimism fluctuates concerning the degree of accuracy actually achievable. The identification of false positives where violence or danger is predicted, but does not come to pass, is more likely than missing cases where it will happen. Risk assessment schedules are not universally popular, and have a poor history of predictive validity, but improvements in practice may still be possible if new procedures are used in conjunction with risk management policies and existing assessment practices.

(4) Serious ethical issues are raised by research on predicting danger, and this is particularly the case in child protection work where the choices are likely to be between unattractive courses of action. Being wrongly identified as dangerous (being 'labelled') could have multiple negative implications including increased dangerousness, and balancing civil liberties with the rights of the child to be protected is critical.

(5) A range of empirical studies of varying quality have identified a number of different factors which may be important in identifying potential perpetrators of violence or other types of dangerous behaviour (the focus has usually been on violence). These relate primarily to past behaviours and events (previous violence and criminal offending, demographic factors, past mental health and personality disorder, personal history) and to present risk factors (substance abuse, current symptomatology and compliance with medication, personal, cognitive and dispositional factors, the decision to use violence, perceptions of children).

(6) Victimisation has received a great deal of attention since the 1980s, and there is a relatively new interest in the role of victim factors and the relationship between the perpetrator and the victim in predicting future events. However, that said, there is a lack of information about the personal and situational risk factors for children

who may be more likely to be the victim of abuse or neglect. Some research has highlighted certain characteristics of children in danger (being of younger age, being premature and/or of low birth weight, being disabled, or more temperamentally difficult), and the role of the child's own account is discussed. Research on situational factors has suggested a role for family problems, low levels of social support, socioeconomic stresses, access to the child, final stressful triggers, and organisational factors. The development of interactional perspectives is discussed, bringing together carer, child and context characteristics.

(7) A range of existing predictive schemes was discussed, aimed at predicting some aspect of violence or dangerous behaviour. There are reasons for being critical of such schemes, but the most productive model in the context of child protection is likely to be one intended to operate as an aide memoire in addition to existing procedures to ensure that all the relevant information has been considered. Most of the schemes are from the US, and there is little evaluative evidence relating to existing UK procedures for assessing carers. The importance of evaluation is stressed.

(8) While the 1970s and 1980s witnessed a rather negative collective view of intervention with violent and dangerous people, current reviews and meta-analyses are rather more positive about the possibilities of reducing risk. Various intervention programmes may have a part to play in reducing recidivism and future dangerousness. From a different angle, there is a fair amount of information on the success of social workers in working with families where child protection issues have been identified, at least in terms of repeated serious abuse, but there is also research showing that intervention often does not prevent abuse of a less serious nature. The importance of risk management was stressed. Key elements of training programmes for professionals assessing dangerousness are likely to include discussions of biases in decision-making, understanding the limits of prediction and the role of structural disadvantage and stereotyping, and being clear on the organisational context.

CONCLUSIONS

Both in the criminological and child protection literatures, the notion of dangerousness has turned out to be a rather difficult concept, even, some have suggested, dangerous (Scott, 1977). Strong political overtones and the policy context tend to make it an emotive topic, and nowhere is this clearer than when it is raised in relation to children. Despite the fact that the term has been in use within the child protection literature for some time, only very limited progress has been made towards clarifying what is meant by it. Operationalising the notion in the context of protection of children without infringing rights or increasing risks remains a serious difficulty. Decisions in child protection are always difficult, given that they are very likely to carry at least some negative consequences. Because much of the dangerousness literature has developed from the mental health and forensic fields, much of it focuses on the placement of adults back in society rather than the removal of children from the home, and is thus of only limited relevance. The pressure to get it right is at least as great if not greater for those working in child protection as in other fields, and while the 1989 Children Act provides a clear legislative framework within which to operate it cannot resolve many of the underlying conflicts which exist between the state and the family, or between individual children and their parents.

This review has shown that very few clear winners emerge in terms of a list of factors that are of critical importance in predicting dangerousness, but there is a developing consensus that integrative schemes bringing together individual, dyadic and situational factors, using both actuarial and clinical assessment procedures, are likely to be most fruitful. Risk is frequently contextual and therefore over simplified additive approaches that focus only on perpetrators are likely to miss key indicators of danger. Useful models exist in prediction of violence in mental health settings and child protection could borrow more heavily from this literature. Such models stress the use of schedules as 'aide memoires', within existing and specified risk management policies. What is required is a multi-factorial, multi-dimensional approach which can bring together factors relating to the carer, the child, and the context. Perhaps we can call this the three C's approach. While we cannot be absolutely definite about factors

Summary and Conclusions

which will certainly predict dangerousness, the review has identified some which do recur again and again in different contexts and with different samples, and it is important that this work is disseminated to child protection workers.

This was only a brief literature review, and inevitably we have to conclude by noting that many questions concerning the assessment and prediction of dangerous family situations cannot be adequately answered. One area that certainly needs further development and more rigorous research attention is that concerning the role of external stresses such as resource availability on the successful contribution of risk management.

In fact, further research is needed generally, to continue to marry different disciplinary approaches, and to seek to apply research techniques and findings to the child protection world. Methodological problems are such that they need to retain a high profile in any discussion of particular risk factors. This review reflects, at the end of the day, the lack of clarity inherent in the literature, but the challenge is to draw practical implications in cases where there is any confidence that these can be derived from the empirical base.

Bibliography

Abel, G, Becker, J, Mittleman, M, Cunningham-Rathner, J, Rouleau, J-L, and Murphy, W (1987) 'Self-reported sex crime of non-incarcerated paraphiliacs' *Journal of Interpersonal Violence*, 2/6, 3–25

Aber, J L, Allen, J P, Carlson, V and Cicchetti, D (1989) 'The effects of maltreatment on development during early childhood: recent studies and their theoretical clinical and policy implications' In: D Cicchetti and V Carlson (Eds) *Child Maltreatment: Theory and Research on the Causes and Consequences of Child Abuse and Neglect* New York: Cambridge University Press

Accardo, P and Whitman, B (1990) 'Children of mentally retarded parents' *American Journal of Diseases of Children*, 144 69–70

Ainsworth, M D S (1979) 'Infant-mother attachment' *American Psychologist*, 34, 932–937

Ammerman, R T, Hensen, M, Van Hasselt, V B (1988) The Child Abuse and Neglect Interview Schedule (CANIS) Unpublished

Asdigain, N L and Finkelhor, D (1995) 'What works for children resisting assaults?' *Journal of Interpersonal Violence*, 10(4) 402–418

Bagley, C and Thurston, W E (1996) *Understanding and preventing child sexual abuse Volume 2, Male victims, Adolescents, Adult outcomes and Offender Treatment* Aldershot, Hampshire: Ashgate Publishing Limited

Baird, C (1988) 'Development of risk assessment indices for the Alaska Department of Health and Social Services' In: Tatara T (Ed) *Validation Research in CPS Risk Assessment* Washington DC: American Public Welfare Association

Barnard, K E, Hammond, M A, Booth, C L, Mitchell, S K, and Spieker, S J (1989) 'Assessment of parent-child interaction' In: S K Meisels and J P Shonkoff (Eds) *Handbook of Early Childhood Intervention* New York: Cambridge University Press

Beck-Sander, A (1995) 'Childhood abuse in adult offenders: the role of control in perpetuating cycles of abuse' *The Journal of Forensic Psychiatry*, 6, 486–498

Bell, S M and Ainsworth, M D S (1972) 'Infant crying and maternal responsiveness' *Child Development*, 48, 182–194

Bem, D, and Funder, D (1978) 'Predicting more of the people more of the time: assessing the personality of situations' *Psychological Review*, 85, 485–501

Berger, L S and Dietrich, S G (1979) 'The clinical prediction of dangerousness: the logic of the process' *International Journal of Offender Therapy and Comparative Criminology*, 23: 35–46

Berkowitz, S (1991) Paper presented to the National Center on Child Abuse and Neglect State Liaison Officers Meeting, Washington DC, April 3–5 1991, and cited in Depanfilis and Scannapieco, 1994, op cit

Bingley, W (1997) 'Assessing dangerousness: protecting the interests of patients' *British Journal of Psychiatry* 178 (suppl 32) 28–29

Black, D and Newman, M (1996) 'Children and Domestic Violence: A Review' *Clinical Child Psychology and Psychiatry*, 1, 79–88

Blackburn, R (1980) 'Still not working? A look at recent outcomes in offender rehabilitation' Paper presented at a British Psychological Society meeting (Scottish Branch) on Deviance, Stirling: Scotland

Blackburn, R (1994) *The Psychology of Criminal Conduct: Theory, Research and Practice* Chichester: John Wiley

Blomhoff, S, Seim, S and Friis, S (1990) 'Can prediction of violence among psychiatric inpatients be improved?' *Hospital and Community Psychiatry*, 41 771–775

Booth, T and Booth, W (1994) *Parenting Under Pressure: Mothers and Fathers with Learning Difficulties* Bucks: Open University Press

Booth, T and Booth, W (1996) 'Parental competence and parents with learning difficulties' *Child and Family Social Work*, 1, 81–86

Borum, R (1996) 'Improving the clinical practice of violence risk assessment: Technology, guidelines and training' *American Psychologist*, 9, 945–956

Boswell, G (1995) *Violent Victims* London: The Princes Trust

Boswell, G (1996) *Young and Dangerous* Aldershot, Hants: Avebury

Bowden, P (1996) 'Violence and mental disorder' In N Walker (Ed) *Dangerous People* London: Blackstone Press

Brady, M, Wright, S and Williams, A (1996) 'Expert opinions' *Community Care*, Sept, 22–23

Brearley, C P (1982) *Risk and Social Work*, London: Routledge and Kegan Paul

Briggs, F (1995) *From Victim to Offender: How Child Sexual Abuse Victims Become Offenders*, London: Allen and Unwin

Brody, S A and Tarling, R (1980) *Taking Offenders Out of Circulation*, HORU research study no 64 London: HMSO

Bibliography

Brown, K and Saqi, S (1987) 'Parent-child interaction in abusing families and its possible causes and consequences' In: P Maher (Ed) *Child Abuse: The Educational Perspective* Oxford: Basil Blackwell

Browne, A, and Finkelhor, D (1986) 'Impact of child sexual abuse: A review of the research' *Psychological Bulletin*, 99, 66–77

Browne, K D, and Lynch, M A (1995) 'The nature and extent of child homicide and fatal abuse' *Child Abuse Review*, 4, 309–316

Bullock, R and Little, M (1996) 'Child protection' *Young Minds*, 24, 17–19

Bumby, K M (1996) 'Assessing the cognitive distortions of child molesters and rapists: Development and validation of the MOLEST and RAPE scales' *Sexual Abuse: A Journal of Research and Treatment*, 8, 1, 37–54

Bush (1995) 'Vermont cognitive self-change project' In: McGuire *What Works. Reducing Offending* Chichester: Wiley

Caliso, J A and Milner, J S (1994) 'Childhood history of abuse and child abuse screening' *Child Abuse and Neglect*, 16 647–659

Campbell, J C (1995) *Assessing Dangerousness: Violence by Sexual Offenders, Batterers and Child Abusers* California: Sage

Caron, C and Rutter, M (1991) 'Comorbidity in child psychopathology: Concepts, issues and research strategies' *Journal of Child Psychology and Psychiatry*, 32, 1063–1080

Carson, D (1993) 'Dangerous people: Through a broader conception of "risk" and "danger" to better decisions' *Expert Evidence*, 3 51–69

Ceci, S J and Bruck, M (1995) *Jeopary in the Courtroom: A Scientific Analysis of Children's Testimony* Washington, DC: American Psychological Association

Central Statistical Office (1994) *Social Trends for Children* London: HMSO

Cicchetti, D and Carlson, V (1989) *Child Maltreatment: Theory and Research on the Causes and Consequences of Child Abuse and Neglect*, Cambridge: Cambridge University Press

Clark, D, Fisher, M and McDougall, C (1993) 'A new methodology for assessing the level of risk in incarcerated offenders' *British Journal of Criminology*, 33 436–448

Claussen, A H and Crittenden, P M (1991) 'Physical and psychological maltreatment: relations among type of maltreatment' *Child Abuse and Neglect*, 15, 5–18

Cleaver, H and Freeman, P (1995) *Parental Perspectives in Cases of Suspected Child Abuse* London: HMSO

Cochrane, R, (1971) 'Mental illness in immigrants to England and Wales An analysis of mental hospital admissions 1971' *International Journal of Social Psychiatry*, 12, 25–35

Coleman, R and Cassell, D (1995a) 'Parents who misuse drugs and alcohol' In: Reder, P and Lucey, C (1995) *Assessment of Parenting: Psychiatric and Psychological Contributions* London: Routledge

Coleman, R and Cassell, D (1995b) 'Parents with psychiatric problems' In: Reder, P and Lucey, C (1995) *Assessment of Parenting: Psychiatric and Psychological Contributions* London: Routledge

Conaway, L P and Hansen, D J (1989) 'Social behaviour of physically abused and neglected children: A critical review' *Clinical Psychology Review*, 9, 687–652

Conrad, J P (1984) 'Research and development in corrections Terminating the executioner: How the empiricist can help' *Federal Probation*, XXXXVIII, 59–62

Copas, J, Marshall, P and Tarling, R (1996) *Predicting Reoffending for Discretionary Conditional Release* London: Home Office

Corby, B and Mills, C (1986) 'Child abuse: risks and resources' *British Journal of Social Work*, 16 531–542

Courtney, M, Barth, R, Berrick, J, Brooks, D, Needell, B and Park, L (1996) 'Race and child welfare services: Past research and future directions' *Child Welfare*, LXXV, 99–137

Creighton, S J (1992) *Child Abuse Trends in England and Wales, 1988–1990, and an Overview from 1973–1990* London: NSPCC

Creighton, S J (1995) 'Fatal child abuse – how preventable is it?' *Child Abuse Review*, 4, 318–328

Crittenden, P M and Ainsworth, M D S (1989) 'Childhood maltreatment and attachment theory' In: D Cicchetti and V Carlson (Eds) *Child Maltreatment: Theory and Research on the Causes and Consequences of Child Abuse and Neglect* New York: Cambridge University Press

Dale, P, Davies, M, Morrison, T and Waters, J (1986) *Dangerous Families: Assessment and Treatment of Child Abuse* London: Tavistock Institute

Dalgleish, L I and Drew, E C (1989) 'The relationship of child abuse indicators to the assessment of perceived risk and to the court's decision to separate' *Child Abuse and Neglect* 13 491–506

DePanfilis, D (1996) 'Social isolation of neglectful families: A review of social support assessment and intervention models' *Child Maltreatment*, 1, 37–52

DePanfilis, D and Scannapieco, M (1994) 'Assessing the safety of children at risk of maltreatment: Decision-making models' *Child Welfare*, LXXIII 229–245

Department of Health (1988) *Protecting Children: A Guide for Social Workers Undertaking Comprehensive Assessment* London: HMSO (the 'orange book')

Bibliography

Department of Health, Home Office and Department of Education and Science (1991) *Working Together* London: HMSO

Department of Health (1995) *Child Protection: Messages from Research* London: HMSO

Dhawan, S and Marshall, W (1996) 'Sexual abuse histories of sexual offenders' *Sexual Abuse: A Journal of Research and Treatment*, 8, 7–15

Dobash, R E and Dobash, R D (1992) *Women, Violence and Social Change*, London: Routledge

Dobash, R E, Dobash, R D, Daly, M, and Wilson, M (1992) 'The myth of sexual symmetry in marital violence' *Social Problems*, 39/1: 71–91

Doueck, H, Bronson, D and Levine, M (1992) 'Evaluating risk assessment implementation in child protection: Issues for consideration' *Child Abuse and Neglect*, 16, 637–646

Doueck, H J, Levine, M and Bronson, D E (1993) 'Risk assessment in child protective services: An evaluation of the child at risk field system' *Journal of Interpersonal Violence*, 8, 446–467

Dowdney, L and Skuse, D (1993) 'Parenting provided by mentally retarded adults' *Journal of Child Psychology and Psychiatry Annual Research Review* 34, 25–47

Doyle, C (1996) Current issues in child protection: An overview of the debates in contemporary journals *British Journal of Social Work* 26 565–576

Egeland, B, Carlson, E and Sroufe, L A (1993) 'Resilience as process' *Development and Psychopathology*, 5, 517–528

English, D and Pecora, P (1994) 'Risk assessment as a practice method in child protective services' *Child Welfare LXXIII*, 451–473

Fagan, J (1990) 'Intoxication and aggression' In: M Tonry and J Wilson, (Eds) *Drugs and Crime* Chicago: University of Chicago Press

Falkov, A (1996) *Study of Working Together Part 8 Reports: Fatal Child Abuse and Parental Psychiatric Disorder* London: Department of Health and Social Security

Fanshel, D, Finch, S and Grundy, J (1994) 'Testing the measurement properties of risk assessment instruments in child protective services' *Child Abuse and Neglect*, 18, 1073–1084

Fantuzzo, J, DePaola, L, Lambert, L and Martino, T (1991) 'Effects of interparental violence on the psychological adjustment and competencies of young children' *Journal of Consulting and Clinical Psychology*, 59, 285–265

Farmer, E and Owen, M (1995) *Child Protection Practice: Private Risks and Public Remedies – Decision-making, Intervention and Outcome in Child Protection Work* London: HMSO

Farrington, D (1994) 'Human development and criminal careers' In: M Maguire, R Morgan and R Reiner (Eds) *The Oxford Handbook of Criminology* Oxford: Oxford University Press

Farrington, D (1995) 'The Twelfth Jack Tizard Memorial Lecture: The development of offending and antisocial behaviour from childhood: Key findings from the Cambridge Study in Delinquent Development' *Journal of Child Psychology and Psychiatry*, 36, 929–964

Farrington, D P, Langan, P A and Wikstrom, P H (1994) 'Changes in crime and punishment in America, England and Sweden between the 1989s and the 1990s' *Studies on Crime amd Crime Prevention*, Vol 3, p104–131, Sweden: National Council for Crime Prevention

Field, S (1990) *Trends in Crime and their Interpretation*, London: HMSO

Finkelhor, D (1986) *A Sourcebook on Child Sexual Abuse*, Beverly Hills: Sage

Finkelhor, D, and Browne, A (1986) 'Initial and long-term effects: A conceptual framework' In: D Finkelhor (Ed) *A Source Book on Child Sexual Abuse* Newbury Park, CA: Sage

Fivush, R and Hudson, J (1990) *Knowing and Remembering in Young Children* Cambridge: Cambridge University Press

Floud, J, and Young, W (1981) *Dangerousness and Criminal Justice*, London: Heinemann

Francis, E, (1989) 'Black People: "Dangerousness" and Psychiatric Compulsion' In: A Brack, and C Grinshaw *Mental Health Care in Crisis*, London: Pluto

Francis, E, (1993) 'Psychiatric racism and social police' In: W James, and C Harris, (1993) *Inside Babylon: Caribbean Diaspora in Britain*, London: Verso

Frieze I, and Browne, A (1989) 'Violence in marriage' In: L Ohlin and M Tonry, (Eds) *Family Violence* Chicago: University of Chicago Press

Frodi, A and Smetana, J (1984) 'Abused, neglected, and nonmaltreated preschoolers' ability to discriminate emotions in others: the effects of IQ' *Child Abuse and Neglect*, 8, 459–465

Frude, N (1980) 'Child abuse as aggression' In: N Frude (Ed) *Psychological Approaches to Child Abuse* London: Batsford

Frude, N (1988) 'The physical abuse of children' In: K Howells and C Hollin, (Eds) *Clinical Approaches to Violence* Chichester: Wiley

Garbarino, J and Vondra, J (1987) 'Psychological maltreatment: issues and perspectives' In: M Brassard, B Germain and S Hart (Eds) *Psychological Maltreatment of Children and Youth* New York: Pergamon

Garmezy, N (1994) 'Chronic adversities' In: M Rutter, E Taylor, L Hersov

Bibliography

(Eds) *Child and Adolescent Psychiatry: Modern Approaches* Oxford: Blackwell Scientific Publications

Gath, A (1995) 'Parents with learning disability' In: P Reder and C Lucey (1995) *Assessment of Parenting: Psychiatric and Psychological Contributions* London: Routledge

Gathercole, C E, Craft, M J, McDougall, J, Barnes, H M, and Peck, D F (1968) 'A review of 100 discharges from a special hospital' *British Journal of Criminology*, 8 419–24

Gaudin, J, Polansky, N, Kilpatrick, A and Shilton, P (1996) 'Family functioning in neglectful families' *Child Abuse and Neglect*, 20, 363–377

Gelles, R J (1991) 'Physical violence, child abuse, and child homicide: A continuum of violence or distinct behaviours?' *Human Nature* 2(1), 59–72

Genders E and Morrison S (1996) 'When violence is the norm' In N Walker (Ed) *Dangerous People* London: Blackstone Press

George, C and Main, M (1979) 'Social interaction of young abused children: Approach, avoidance and aggression' *Chid Development*, 50, 306–318

Ghate, D and Spencer, L (1995) *The Prevalence of Child Sexual Abuse in Britain: A Feasibility Study for a Large Scale National Survey of the General Population* London: HMSO

Gibbens, J, Gallagher, B, Bell, C, Gordon, D (1995) *Development after Physical Abuse in Early Childhood – a Follow Up* London: HMSO

Glaser, D (1995) 'Emotionally abusive experiences' In: P Reder and C Lucey *Assessment of Parenting: Psychiatric and Psychological Contributions* London: Routledge

Gloucestershire Area Child Protection Committee (1995) *Part 8 Case Review Overview Report in respect of Charmaine and Heather West* Gloucester: GACPC

Gottfredson, D M and Gottfredson, S D (1988) 'Stakes and risks in the prediction of violent criminal behaviour' *Violence and Victims*, 3, 851–855

Gough, D (1993) *Child Abuse Interventions: A Review of the Research Literature* London: HMSO

Graham, J and Bowling, B (1995) *Young People and Crime* London: HMSO

Greenland, C (1978) 'The prediction and management of dangerous behaviour: Social policy issues' *International Journal of Law and Psychiatry*, 6 391–98

Greenland, C (1980) 'Psychiatry and the prediction of dangerousness' *Journal of Psychiatric Treatment and Evaluation*, 2: 97–103

Griffiths, M (1995) *Adolescent Gambling*, London: Routledge

Groth, A N (1979) 'Sexual trauma in the life histories of rapists and child molesters' *Victimology*, 4, 10–16

Haapanen, R (1990) *Selective Incapacitation and the Serious Offender*, New York: Springer-Verlag

Hagell, A and Newburn, T (1994) *Persistent Young Offenders* London: Policy Studies Institute

Hagen, M P, King, R P and Patros, R L (1994) 'Recidivism among adolescent perpetrators of sexual assault against children' *Journal of Offender Rehabilitation*, 21, 127–137

Hall, H V (1984) 'Predicting dangoursness for the courts' *American Journal of Forensic Psychology* 4, 5–25

Hall, H V (1987) *Violence Prediction: Guidelines for the Forensic Practitioner*, Illinois: Charles C Thomas

Hallett, C and Birchall, E (1992) *Coordination and Child Protection: A Review of the Literature* London: HMSO

Hanson, R K, and Slater, S (1988) 'Sexual victimization in the history of child sexual abusers: A review' *Annals of Sex Research*, 1, 485–499

Harding, T and Adserballe, H (1983) 'Assessments of dangerousness: observations in six countries A summary of results from a WHO co-ordinated study' *International Journal of Law and Psychiatry*, 6, 391–98

Hare, R D (1991) *Manual for the Hare Psychopathy Checklist – Revised*, Toronto, Ontario: Multi-Health Systems

Hare, R D (1993) *Without Conscience: The Disturbing World of the Psychopaths Among Us*, New York: Pocket Books

Harrington, R, Fudge, H, Rutter, M, Pickles, A and Hill, J (1991) 'Adult outcomes of childhood and adolescent depression: II Links with antisocial disorders' *Journal of the American Academy of Child and Adolescent Psychiatry*, 30 434–439

Harris Hendricks, J, Black, D and Kaplan, T (1993) *When Father Kills Mother: Guiding Children through Trauma and Grief* London: Routledge

Hart, S, Hare, R and Forth, A (1994) 'Psychopathy as a risk marker for violence: development and validation of a screening version of the Revised Psychopathy Checklist' In: J Monahan and H Steadman (Eds) *Violence and Mental Disorder: Developments in Risk Assessment* Chicago: University of Chicago Press

Hawkins, K (1983) 'Assessing evil: Decision behaviour and parole board justice' *British Journal of Criminology*, 23, 101–27

Heidenson, F (1995) 'Gender and crime' In: M Maguire, R Morgan and R Reiner (Eds) *The Oxford Handbook of Criminology* Oxford: Oxford University Press

Herzberger, S D, Potts, D A and Dillon, M (1981) 'Abusive and non-abusive parental treatment from the child's perspective' *Journal of Consulting and Clinical Psychology*, 49, 81–90

Hinton, J W (1975) 'Development of objective behaviour rating scales for use by nurses on patients in special hospitals' *Special Hospitals Reseach Reports*, No 13: London

Hinton, J W (1983a) 'Behaviour rating of 'dangerous patients'' In: J Hinton (Ed) *Dangerousness: Problems of Assessment and Prediction*, London: George Allen and Unwin

Hinton, J W (1983b) *Dangerousness: Problems of Assessment and Prediction*, London: George Allen and Unwin

Hoffman-Plotkin, D and Twentyman, C (1984) 'A multi modal assessment of behavioural and cognitive deficits in abused and neglected pre-schoolers' *Child Development*, 52, 34–64

Hollin, C R (1989) *Psychology and Crime: An Introduction to Criminological Psychology*, London: Routledge

Hollin, C R, Epps, K and Kendrick, D J (1995) *Managing Behaviour Treatment: Policy and Practice with Delinquent Adolescents* London: Routledge

Home Office (1995) *Criminal Statistics* London: HMSO

Home Office and DHSS (1975) *Report of the Committee on Mentally Abnormal Offenders (Butler Committee)* Cmnd 6244 London: HMSO

Howells, K (1987) 'Forensic problems: investigation' In: S Lindsay and C Powell (Eds) *A Handbook of Clinical Adult Psychology* London: Gower

Hunter, M (1990) *The Sexually Abused Male: Prevalence, Impact and Treatment*, Lexington, MA: D C Heath

Hurley, D J and Jaffe, P (1990) 'Children's observations of violence:II Clinical implications for children's mental health professionals' *Canadian Journal of Psychiatry*, 35, 471–476

Iverson, T J, Tanner, S L and Segal, M (1987) 'Assessing abused and neglected children's social interactions with the behaviour observation record' Nova University, unpublished manuscript

Iwaniec D (1995) *The emotionally abused and neglected child: Identification, assessment and intervention* Chichester: Wiley

Jacobson, R S and Straker, G (1982) 'Peer group interaction of physically abused children' *Child Abuse and Neglect*, 16, 210–265

Jagannathan, R and Camasso, M (1996) 'Risk assessment in child protective services: A canonical analysis of the case management function' *Child Abuse and Neglect*, 20, 599–612

Jeyarajah Dent, R (Ed) (1998) *Dangerous Care – Working to Protect Children* London: The Bridge Child Care Development Service

Kandel, D and Mednick, S A (1991) 'Perinatal complications predict violent offending' *Criminology*, 29, 519–530

Kaufman, J, and Zigler, E (1987) 'Do abused children become abusive parents?' *American Journal of Orthopsychiatry*, 57, 186–192

Keane, C, Gillis, A and Hagan, J (1989) 'Deterrence and amplification of juvenile delinquency by police contact' *British Journal of Criminology*, 29, 336–352

Kelly, N and Milner, J (1996) 'Child protection decision-making' *Child Abuse Review*, 5, 91–102

Kemshall, H (1995a) 'Offender risk and probation practice' In: H Kemshall and J Pritchard (1995) *Good Practice in Risk Assessment and Risk Management* Jessica Kingsley

Kemshall, H (1995b) 'Risk in probation practice' *Probation Journal*, 42

Kemshall, H (1996) *Reviewing Risk: A Review of Research on the Assessment and Management of Risk and Dangerousness: Implications for Policy and Practice in the Probation Service* London: Home Office

Kemshall, H and Pritchard, J (1995) *Good Practice in Risk Assessment and Risk Management* Jessica Kingsley

Kendall-Tackett, K, Williams, L M, and Finkelhor, D (1993) 'Impact of sexual abuse on children: A review and synthesis of recent empirical studies' *Psychological Bulletin*, 113, 164–180

Kozol, H L, Boucher, R J, and Garofalo, R F (1972) 'The Diagnosis and Treatment of Dangerousness' *Crime and Delinquency*, 18, 371–92

Kropp, P R, Hart, S D, Webster, C D, and Eaves, D Anonymous (1994) *Manual for the Spousal Assault Risk Assessment Guide*, Vancouver, BC: The British Columbia Institute on Family Violence

Langevin, R, Wright, P, and Handy L (1989) 'Characteristics of sex offenders who were sexually victimised as children' *Annals of Sex Research*, 2, 227–253

Lawson, B, Masson, H, and Milner, J (1995) '"There but for the Grace…?" Developing multi-disciplinary training following a local child death inquiry' *Child Abuse Review*, 4, 340–350

LeBlanc, C and Loeber, R (1991) 'Temporal paths in delinquency: stability, regression and progression analysed with panel data from an adolescent and a delinquent male sample' *Canadian Journal of Criminology* 23–44

Leonard, E (1996) 'A social exchange explanation for the child sexual abuse accommodation syndrome' *Journal of Interpersonal Violence*, 11, 107–117

Levi, M (1994) 'Violent Crime' In: M Maguire, R Morgan, and R Reiner (Eds) *The Oxford Handbook of Criminology* Oxford: Oxford University Press

Limandri, B and Sheridan, D J (1995) 'Prediction of intentional interpersonal violence: An introduction' In: J Campbell *Assessing Dangerousness* Thousand Oaks: Sage

Link, BG, Andrews H and Cullen FT (1992) 'Violent and illegal behaiour of mental patients reconsidered' *American Sociological Review*, 57, 275–292

Link BG and Stueve A (1994) 'Psychotic symptoms and violent/illegal behaviour of mental patients compared to community controls' In Monahan J and Steadman H (1994) (Eds) *Violence and Mental disorder: Developments in Risk Assessment* Chicago: University of Chicago Press

Little, M et al (unpublished)

Litz, C W, Mulvey, E P and Gardner, W (1993) 'The accuracy of predictions of violence to others' *Journal of the American Medical Association*, 269, 1007–1011

Livermore, J, Malmquist, C and Meehl, P (1968) 'On the justification for civil commitment' *University of Pensylvania Law Review*, 117: 75–96

Lloyd, C, Mair, G and Hough, M (1994) *Explaining Reconviction Rates: A Critical Analysis* London: HMSO

Loeber, R and Dishion, T (1983) 'Early predictors of male delinquency: A review' *Psychological Bulletin*, 94 68–99

Loeber, R and Hay, D F (1994) 'Developmental approaches to aggression and conduct problems' In: M Rutter and D Hay (Eds) *Development Through Life: A Handbook for Clinicians* Oxford: Blackwell Scientific

Losel, F (1995) 'The efficiency of correctional treatment: A review and synthesis of meta-evaluations' In J McGuire (Ed) *What works: Reducing offending* Chichester: Wiley

Lytton, H (1990) 'Child and parent effects in boys' conduct disorder: A reinterpretation' *Developmental Psychology*, 26, 683–697

McDonald, T and Marks, J (1991) 'A review of risk factors assessed in child protective services' *Social Service Review*, 112–132

McDonald, K I (1995) 'Comparative homicide and the proper aims of social work: a sceptical note' *British Journal of Social Work* 25, (4)

McDonald, T and Marks, J (1991) 'A review of risk factors assessed in child protective services' *Social Service Review*, March, 113–131

McGuire J (1995) *What works: Reducing offending* Chichester: Wiley

McNeil, D E and Binder, RL (1994) 'Screening for risk of inpatient violence: Validation of an actuarial tool' *Law and Human Behaviour*, 18, 579–586

Maguire, M, Pionter, F, and Collis, C (1984) 'Dangerousness and the tariff' *British Journal of Criminology*, 24, 250–268

Main, M and George, C (1985) 'Responses to abused and disadvantaged toddlers to distress in age mates: a study in the day care setting' *Developmental Psychology*, 21, 407–412

Malinosky-Rummell, R and Hansen, D (1993) 'Long-term consequences of childhood physical abuse' *Psychological Bulletin*, 114, 68–79

Mastern A S, Best, K M and Garmezy, N (1990) 'Resilience and development: contributions from the study of children who overcome adversity' *Development and Psychopathology*, 2, 425–444

Martinson, R (1974) 'What works? Questions and answers about prison reform' *The Public Interest*, 35, 22–54

Megargee, E (1976) 'The prediction of dangerous behaviour' *Criminal Justice and Behaviour*, 3, 3–22

Menzies, R, Webster, C D, McMain, S, Staley, S, and Scaglione, R (1994) 'The dimensions of dangerousness revisited' *Law and Human Behaviour*, 18, (1) 1–20

Milner, J S (1995) 'Physical child abuse assessment: Perpetrator evaluation' In: J Campbell *Assessing Dangerousness* Thousand Oaks: Sage

Milner, J S and Chilamkurti, C (1991) 'Physical child abuse perpetrator characteristics: A review of the literature' *Journal of Interpersonal Violence* 6, 345–366

Milner, J S and Foody, R (1993) unpublished manuscript cited in Milner, 1995 op cit

Milner, J S, Robertson, I C R and Rogers, D L (1990) 'Childhood history of abuse and adult abuse potential' *Journal of Family Violence*, 5, 15–34

Mirlees-Black, C, Mayhew, P and Percy, A (1996) *The 1996 British Crime Survey: England and Wales* Home Office Statistical Bulletin 19/96, London: Home Office

Modestin, J and Ammann, R (1995) 'Mental disorders and criminal behaviour' *British Journal of Psychiatry*, 166, 667–675

Moffitt, T (1993) 'The neuropsychology of conduct disorder' *Development and Psychopathology* 5, 135–151

Monahan, J, (1981), *Predicting Violent Behaviour: An Asessment of Clinical Techniques*, Beverley Hills: Sage

Monahan, J, (1984), 'The prediction of violent behaviour: Toward a second generation of theory and policy' *American Journal of Psychiatry*, 141 (1) 10–15

Monahan, J (1988) 'Risk assessment of violence among the mentally disordered: Generating useful knowledge' *International Journal of Law and Psychiatry*, 11, 249–257

Monahan, J, and Klassen, D (1982) 'Situational approaches to understanding and predicting individual violent behaviour' In: M Wolfgang and N Weiner (Eds) *Criminal Violence* Beverley Hills: Sage

Monahan, J and Steadman, H (1994) 'Towards a rejuvenation of risk assessment research' in Monahan J and Steadman H (1994) (Eds) *Violence and Mental Disorder: Developments in Risk Assessment* Chicago: University of Chicago Press

Monahan, J and Steadman, H (1994) (Eds) *Violence and Mental disorder: Developments in Risk Assessment* Chicago: University of Chicago Press

Moncher, F, (1995) 'Social isolation and child-abuse risk' Families in Society: *The Journal of Contemporary Human Services*, 421–433

Monck, E and New, M (1996) *Report of a Study of Sexually Abused Children and Adolescents, and of Young Perpetrators of Sexual Abuse Who Were Treated in Voluntary Agency Community Facilities* London: HMSO

Moncrieff, J, Drummond, D, Candy, B, Checinski, K and Farmer, R (1996) 'Sexual abuse in people with alcohol problems: A study of the prevalence of sexual abuse and its relationship to drinking behaviour' *British Journal of Psychiatry, 169*, 355–360

Montanden, C and Harding, T (1984) 'The reliability of dangerousness assesments: A decision-making exercise' *British Journal of Psychiatry*, 144: 145–49

Morris, N and Miller, M (1985) 'Predictions of Dangerousness' In: M Tonry and N Morris (Eds) *Crime and Justice: An Annual Review of Research* Chicago: University of Chicago Press

Morisset, C E, Barnard, K E, Greenberg, M T, Booth, C L, and Spieker, S J (1990) 'Environmental influences on early language development: The context of social risk' *Development and Psychopathology*, 2 127–149

Mossman, D (1994) 'Assessing predictions of violence: Being accurate about accuracy' *Journal of Consulting and Clinical Psychology, 62*, 783–792

Mullen, P E, Martin, J L, Anderson, J C, Romans, S E and Herbison, G P (1993) 'Childhood sexual abuse and mental health in adult life' *British Journal of Psychiatry*, 163, 721–732

Mullen, P E, Martin, J C, Anderson, J C, Romans S E and Herbison, G P (1996) 'The long term impact of the physical, emotional and sexual abuse of children: A community study' *Journal of Abuse and Neglect*, 20, (1) 7–21

Murphy-Berman, V (1994) 'A conceptual framework for thinking about risk assessment and case management in child protective service' *Child Abuse and Neglect, 18*, 193–201

Newman, M, Black, D and Harris Hendricks, J (1996 in press) 'Child victims of disaster, war or homicide: Psychological effects on siblings' *Journal of Child Psychology and Psychiatry*

O'Keefe, M (1996) 'The differential effects of family violence on adolescent adjustment' *Child and Adolescent Social Work Journal* 13, p51–68

Oldershaw, L, Walters, G and Hall, D (1986) Control strategies and noncompliance in abusive mother-child dyads; an observational study' *Child Development*, 57, 722–732

Olds, D L, Henderson, C R, Chamberlin, R and Tatelbaum, R (1986) 'Preventing child abuse and neglect: a randomized trial of nurse home visitation' *Pediatrics*, 78, 65–78

Owen, M and Farmer E (1996) 'Child protection in a multi-racial context' *Policy and Politics*, 24, 299–313

Pan, H, Neidig, P and O'Leary, K (1994) 'Predicting mild and severe husband-to-wife physical aggression' *Journal of Consulting and Clinical Psychology*, 62, 975–981

Parton (1991) *Governing the Family: Child Care, Child Protection and the State*

Patterson, G R, DeBaryshe, B D and Ramsey, E (1989) 'A developmental perspective on antisocial behaviour' *American Psychologist*, 44, 329–225

Payne, C, McCabe, S, and Walker, N (1974) 'Predicting offender-patients' reconvictions' *British Journal of Psychiatry*, 125, 60–4

Peay, J (1982) '"Dangerousness" – Ascription or Description?' In: P Feldman (Ed) *Developments in the Study of Criminal Behaviour* Chichester: John Wiley and Sons

Pecora, P J (1991) 'Investigating allegations of child maltreatment: The strengths and limitations of current risk assessment systems' In: *Assessing Child Maltreatment Reports* Haworth Press

Petrunik, M (1982) 'The Politics of Dangerousness' *International Journal of Law and Psychiatry*, 5, 225–53

Pfohl, S J (1979) 'From whom will we be protected? Comparative Aproaches to the Assessment of Dangerousness' *International Journal of Law and Psychiatry*, 3, 55–78

Prentky, R A, Knight, R A, Sims-Knight, J E, Strauss, H, Rokous, F, Cerce, D (1989) 'Developmental antecedents of sexual aggression' *Development and Psychopathology*, 1, 153–169

Prins, H (1986) *Dangerous Behaviour, the Law, and Mental Disorder*, London: Tavistock

Quinsey, V L (1979) 'Assessments of the dangerousness of mental patients held in maximum security' *International Journal of Law and Psychiatry*, 2, 389–406

Quinsey, V L (1980) 'The base rate problem and the prediction of dangerousness: a reappraisal' *Journal of Psychiatry and Law*, 8, 329–340

Quinsey, V L, Pruesse, M, and Fernley, R (1975) 'Oak-Ridge patients: prerelease characteristics and post-release adjustment' *Journal of Psychiatry and Law*, Spring: 63–77

Raine (in press) 'Antisocial behaviour and psychophysiology: A biosocial perspective and a prefrontal dysfunction hypothesis' In: D Stoff, J Breiling and J D Maser (Eds) *Handbook of Antisocial Behaviour*

Reder, P (1998) Research findings – from 'Beyond Blame' to 'Part 8 Enquiries' Paper presented at BASPCAN conference 'Aspects of Risk Assessment' UMIST Conference Centre, Manchester, 18 May

Reder, P, Duncan, S and Gray, M (1993) *Beyond Blame: Child Abuse Tragedies Revisited* London: Routledge

Reder, P and Fitzpatrick, G (1995) 'Assessing the needs of siblings following a child abuse death' *Child Abuse Review*, 4, 382–388

Reder, P and Lucey, C (1995) *Assessment of Parenting: Psychiatric and Psychological Contributions* London: Routledge

Robins, L N (1966) *Deviant Children Grown Up* Baltimore: Williams and Wilkins

Robins, L N (1978) 'Sturdy childhood predictors of adult antisocial behaviour: replications from longitudinal studies' *Psychological Medicine*, 8, 611–622

Robins, L N (1991) 'Conduct disorder' *Journal of Child Psychology and Psychiatry*, 32, 193–212

Robins, L N and Rutter, M (1990) *Straight and Devious Pathways from Childhood to Adulthood* Cambridge: Cambridge University Press

Rodwell, M K and Chambers, D E (1992) 'Primary prevention of child abuse: Is it really possible?' *Journal of Sociology and Social Welfare* 19(3) 159–176

Rogers, C N, and Terry, T (1984) 'Clinical interventions with boy victims of sexual abuse' In: I R Stuart and J G Greer (Eds) *Victims of Sexual Aggression: Treatment of Children, Women and Men* New York: Van Nostrand Reinhold

Rosenstein, P (1995) 'Parental levels of empathy as related to risk assessment in child protective services' *Child Abuse and Neglect, 11,* 1349–1360

Rowe, D (1983) 'Biometrical genetic models of self-reported delinquent behaviour: A twin study' *Behaviour Genetics* 13, 473–489

Royal College of Psychiatrist Special Working Party on Clinical Assessment and Management of Risk (1996) *Assessment and Clinical Management of Risk of Harm to Other People* Leaflet, RCP: London

Russell, D E H (1983) 'The incidence and prevalence of intrafamilial sexual abuse of female children' *Child Abuse and Neglect*, 7, 133–146

Rutter, M (1983) 'Stress coping and development: some issues and some questions' In: N Garmezy and M Rutter (Eds) *Stress, Coping and Development in Young Children* New York: Mcgraw Hill

Rutter, M (1989) 'Intergenerational continuities and discontinuities' In: D Cicchetti and V Carlson (Eds) *Child Maltreatment: Theory and Research on the Causes and Consequences of Child Abuse and Neglect* New York: Cambridge University Press

Rutter, M (1996) 'Hetereogeneity of antisocial behaviour: Causes, continuities, and consequences' Paper presented at the 44th Annual Nebraska Symposium on Motivation

Rutter, M, Giller, H and Hagell, A (1998) *Antisocial Behaviour by Young People* New York: Cambridge University Press

Rutter, M, Harrington, R, Quinton, D and Pickles, A (1994) 'Adult outcome of conduct disorders in childhood: implications for concepts and definitions of psychopathology' In: R D Ketterlinus and M E Lamb (Eds) *Adolescent Problem Behaviours: Issues and Research* Hillsdale NH: Lawrence Erlbaum Associates

Sampson, R and Laub, J H (1993) *Crime in the Making: Pathways and Turning Points* Cambridge, Mass: Harvard University Press

Scott, P D (1977) 'Assessing Dangerousness in Criminals' *British Journal of Psychiatry*, 131: 127–42

Sebold, J (1987) 'Indicators of child sexual abuse in males' *Social Casework: The Journal of Contemporary Social Work*, 68, 75–80

Seghorn, T K, Prentky, R A and Boucher, R J (1987) 'Childhood sexual abuse in the lives of sexually aggressive offenders' *Journal of American Child and Adolescent Psychiatry*, 26, 262–267

Sepejak, D, Menzies, R, Webster, C D, and Jensen, F A S (1983) 'Clinical predictions of dangerousness: Two-year follow-up of 408 pre-trial forensic cases' *Bulletin of the AAPL*, 11 (2) 171–181

Shah, S A (1981) 'Legal and Mental Health System Interactions: Major Developments and Research Needs' *International Journal of Law and Psychiatry*, 4, 219–70

Sharland, E, Jones, D, Aldgate, J, Seal, H and Croucher, M (1995) *Professional Intervention in Child Sexual Abuse* London: HMSO

Sheppard, C (1971) 'The violent offender: Let's examine the taboo' *Federal Probation*, 4, 12–19

Simon, R I (1995) 'Legal and ethical issues' In: E Hollander and D Stein (1995) *Impulsivity and Agression*, New York: Wiley

Skuse, D and Bentovim, A (1994) 'Physical and emotional maltreatment' In: M Rutter, E Taylor and L Hersov (Eds) *Child and Adolescent Psychiatry: Modern Approaches* Oxford: Blackwell Scientific Publications

Smith, C, Lizotte, A J, Thornberry, T and Krohn, M D (1995) 'Resilient youth: Identifying factors that prevent high-risk youth from engaging in delinquency and drug use' In: J Hagan (Ed) *Delinquency and Disrepute in the Life Course* Greenwich, CT: JAI Press

Smith, D J (1995) 'Youth crime and conduct disorders: Trends, patterns and causal explanations' In: M Rutter and D J Smith (Eds) *Psychosocial Disorders in Young People: Time trends and their causes* Chichester: Wiley

Snyder, H N and Sickmund, M (1995) *Juvenile Offenders* Washington USA: National Institute of Justice

Snyder, H N, Sickmond, M and Poe-Yamagata, E (1996) *Juvenile Offenders and Victims: 1996 Update on Violence* Pittsburgh PA: National Center for Juvenile Justice

Soothill, K L, Way, C K and Gibbens, T C N (1980) 'Subsequent dangerousness among compulsory hospital patients' *British Journal of Criminology*, 20: 289–295

Spencer, D and Flin, R (1993) *The Evidence of Children: The Law and the Psychology Second Edition*, London: Blackstone Press

Sroufe, L A (1983) 'Infant caregiver attachment and patterns of adaptation in the preschool: The roots of maladaption and competence' In: M Perlmutter (Ed) *Minnesota Symposium in Child Psychology*, 16, 41–83

Steadman, H J (1976) 'Predicting dangerousness' In: D J Madden and J R Lion (Eds) *Rage, Hate, Assault and Other Forms of Violence*, New York: Spectrum

Steadman, H J (1982) 'A situational approach to violence' *International Journal of Law and Psychiatry*, 5, 171–86

Steadman, H J (1983) 'Predicting dangerousness among the mentally ill: Art, magic and science' *International Journal of Law and Psychiatry*, 6, 381–90

Steadman, H J, and Cocozza, J J (1974) *Careers of the Criminally Insane: Excessive Social Control of Deviance*, Lexington, MA: Lexington Books

Stone, M (1992) *A model for risk assessment in physical abuse/neglect* London

Suedfeld, P (1980) 'Environmental effects on violent behaviour in prisons' *International Journal of Offender Therapy and Comparative Criminology*, 24

Sumner, M and Parker, H (1995) *Low in Alcohol* The Portman Group: London

Swanson, J W (1994) 'Mental disorder, substance abuse and community violence: An epidemiological approach' in J Monahan and H Steadman (1994, Eds) *Violence and Mental disorder: Developments in Risk Assessment* Chicago: University of Chicago Press

Swanson, J W and Holzer, C E (1991) 'Violence and the ECA data' *Hospital and Community Psychiatry*, 42, 79–80

Swanson, J W, Holzer, C E, Ganju, V K and Jono, R T (1990) 'Violence and psychiatric disorder in the community: Evidence from the Epidemiologic Catchment Area Surveys' *Hospital and Community Psychiatry, 41,* 761–770

Tallant, C, and Strachan, R (1995) 'The importance of framing: A pragmatic approach to risk assessment' *Probation Journal,* December, 202–207

Taylor, P, Garety, P, Buchanan, A, Reed, A, Westley, S, Ray, K, Dunn, G and Grubin, D (1994) 'Delusions and violence' In: J Monahan and H Steadman (Eds) *Violence and Mental Disorder: Developments in Risk Assessment* Chicago: University of Chicago Press

Thoburn, J, Lewis, A and Shemmings, D *Paternalism or Partnership? Family Involvement in the Child Protection Process* London: HMSO

Thornberry, T P, and Jacoby, J E (1979) *The Criminally Insane: A Community Follow-up of Mentally Ill Offenders,* Chicago, IL: University of Chicago Press

Thornberry, T P, Huizinga, D and Loeber, R (1995) 'The prevention of serious delinquency and violence: implications from the program of research on the causes and correlates of delinquency' In J C Howell, B Krisberg, J D Hawkins and J J Wilson (Eds) *Sourcebook on Serious, Violent and Chronic Juvenile Offenders* Thousand Oaks, CA: Sage Publications

Tidmarsh, D (1982) 'Implications from research studies' In: J R Hamilton and H Freeman (Eds) *Dangerousness: Psychiatric Assessment and Management,* London: Gaskell

Tong, E and Mackay, G W (1959) 'A statistical follow-up of mental defectives of dangerous and violent propensities' *British Journal of Delinquency,* IX: 276–84

Trickett, P K, Aber, J L, Carlson, V and Cicchetti, D (1991) Relationship of socioeconomic status to the etiology and developmental sequelne of physical child abuse *Developmental Psychology 27,* 148–158

Trickett, P K and McBride-Chang, C, (1995) 'The developmental impact of different forms of child abuse and neglect' *Developmental Review,* 15, 331–337

Vizard, E, Monck, E, and Misch, P (1995) 'Child and adolescent sex abuse perpetrators: A review of the research literature' *Journal of Child Psychology and Psychiatry, 36,* (5) 731–756

Walker, M (1995) *Interpreting Crime Statistics* Oxford: Clarendon Press

Walker, N (1978) 'Dangerous people' *International Journal of Law and Psychiatry,* 11, 37–50

Walker, N (1996) *Dangerous People* London: Blackstone Press

Bibliography

Waterhouse, L and Carnie, J (1992) Assessing child protection risk *British Journal of Social Work* 22, 47–60

Watkins, B, and Bentovim, A (1992) 'The sexual abuse of male children and dolescents: A review of current research' *Journal of Child Psychology and Psychiatry*, *33*, 197–248

Webster, C (1995) *The Prediction of Dangerousness and the Assessment of Risk in Mentally and Personality Disordered Individuals*, Conference Paper, Faculty of Law, University of Southampton

Webster, C D, Ben-Aron, M H, and Hucker, S J (1985) *Dangerousness: Probability and Prediction, Psychiatry and Public Policy* Cambridge: Cambridge University Press

Webster, C D and Eaves, D (1995) *The HRC-20 Scheme: The Assessment of Dangerousness and Risk* British Columbia: Simon Fraser University

Webster, C D, Harris, G T, Rice, M E, Cormier, C and Quinsey, V L (1994) *The Violence Prediction Scheme: Assessing Dangerousness in High Risk Men*, Toronto: Centre of Criminology, University of Toronto

Whissell, C, Lewko, J, Carriere, R and Radford, J (1990) 'Test scores and sociodemographic information as predictors of child abuse potential scores in young female adults' *Journal of Social Behaviour and Personality*, *5*, 199–208

White, R (1995) 'A perspective from child death reviews' *Child Abuse Review* 4, 365–370

Widom, C (1989) 'Does violence beget violence? A critical examination of the literature' *Psychological Bulletin*, *106*, 3–28

Wiffin, J (1996) 'Clear and present danger' *Community Care*, 25 April–1 May

Wyatt, G E and Peters, S D (1986) Methodological considerations in research on the prevalence of child sexual abuse *Child Abuse and Neglect* 10, 241–251

Zahn-Waxler, C (1993) 'Warriors and worriers: Gender and psychopathology' *Development and Psychopathology*, 5, 79–90

Zoccolillo, M (1993) 'Gender and the development of conduct disorder' *Development and Psychopathology* 5, 65–78